Property of L
700 Fifth St
Laurel, Md 20707

75

W9-CDE-938

PAST
LIVES
THERAPY

PAST
LIVES
THERAPY

by MORRIS NETHERTON, Ph.D.
and NANCY SHIFFRIN

Preface by WALTER STEISS, M.D.

WILLIAM MORROW AND COMPANY, INC.
NEW YORK   1978

Copyright © 1978 by Morris Netherton, Nancy Shiffrin, and Jack Viertel

In all of the case histories cited, the authors have used fictitious names and described traits not identifiable to any particular person or persons.

All rights reserved. No part of this book may be reproduced or utilized in any form or by any means, electronic or mechanical, including photocopying, recording or by any information storage and retrieval system, without permission in writing from the Publisher. Inquiries should be addressed to William Morrow and Company, Inc., 105 Madison Ave., New York, N. Y. 10016.

Library of Congress Cataloging in Publication Data

Netherton, Morris.
    Past lives therapy.

    Bibliography: p.
    1. Reincarnation therapy. I. Shiffrin, Nancy
joint author. II. Title
RC489.R43N47   615'.851   77-29262
ISBN 0-688-03298-2

BOOK DESIGN   CARL WEISS

Printed in the United States of America.

First Edition

1 2 3 4 5 6 7 8 9 10

FOR MY WIFE

CAROL JOYCE

*who found out that it really was worth it
while I was finding out that it could be done*

—MORRIS NETHERTON

ACKNOWLEDGMENTS

I'd like to acknowledge Jack Viertel for his very special contribution to this work, Jill Landesfeld, former associate editor at *Human Behavior,* for her assistance in researching reincarnation, Jack Lent for planting the seed, and David Bean for his faithful friendship during the rough times.

—NANCY SHIFFRIN

PREFACE

THE AWARE PHYSICIAN MUST BE ALERT TO ANY DEVELOPMENT that will enlarge his understanding. When a new method of treatment consistently gets impressive results, it is the responsibility of every doctor to take notice.

I've known Morris Netherton as a colleague and friend for six years. During this time I have become more and more impressed with the work he has done in a technique called Past Lives Therapy. I am pleased and excited that Dr. Netherton has decided to compile his findings in book form. Although the doctrine of reincarnation is used as a tool in this therapy, belief in reincarnation is not essential to its success. Nonetheless, it has taken courage and conviction for Dr. Netherton to pursue this work in the face of almost certain cynicism from some segments of the public. I think he cannot help but be rewarded for carrying out this work; those with open minds will agree that the results speak for themselves.

Past Lives Therapy works on the assumption that patients can trace this life's trauma, both mental and physical, to roots in past lives. It is a technique for erasing the effects of these incidents, so that an individual can learn to live in the present. This book deals with the psychological implications of the therapy. As a physician, I feel that the technique can broaden our view of mental and physiological disease.

From the medical point of view, the most interesting thing about Past Lives Therapy is that it establishes the connection between mind and body. Most doctors accept the fact that the mind profoundly affects the body; this is readily apparent in such diseases as ulcers and migraines. What is less frequently realized is that a psychological component exists for every physical disease. Medical researchers are now beginning to explore this area, most notably in the case of cancer, where a personality profile for that disease is emerging.

In Past Lives Therapy we find that the converse is also true. For every psychological problem, patients can identify a physical injury in past life. Body and mind exist in a reciprocal relationship which makes it essential to probe the effects of one upon the other.

Dr. Netherton does not claim that Past Lives Therapy eliminates the need for medical treatment. It cannot cure a physical condition which has already damaged the body. But doctors often observe that physically sick people have a psychological need for their diseases. Past Lives Therapy can help an individual see where the need for his disease comes from, and enable him to let go of it. It is extremely effective in limiting physical pain as well. Pain is a subjective experience; a given condition may hurt one patient much more than another. Past Lives Therapy demonstrates that physical pain is tied to past experiences. It can be eased by detaching a patient from this past trauma, frequently eliminating the need for debilitating, habit-forming, pain-killing drugs.

Past Lives Therapy has implications for the medical management of pregnancy, birth, and death, three important times in the life cycle that usually fall under the doctor's jurisdiction. Medical research is beginning to show that the unborn child has more awareness than had previously been recognized. It can be demonstrated that the fetus responds to light, sound, and the feelings of the mother. Dr. Netherton's work, bringing people through their prenatal and birth experiences, supports and expands this research with personal stories of remarkable prenatal and childbirth memory.

This therapy has much to contribute to the understanding of death as well. Fear of death, and the concomitant discomfort most feel in the presence of the dying, is eased through the exploration of deaths in past lives. The working through of these incidents, whether or not accompanied by a literal belief in life after death, can resolve the situation for both the dying person and his family.

Finally, because it is so effective with children, and because they take to it so readily, Past Lives Therapy has implications for early prevention of emotional and physical problems.

This book represents Dr. Netherton's work at a midpoint. He has brought to our attention a technique that is, of itself, complete. It makes people healthier, risking none of the side effects of drug use. It is, in other words, ideal treatment. I believe, moreover, that the implications of what Dr. Netherton is doing are vast. I would invite both medical and psychological researchers to test the findings of Past Lives Therapy. The data produced could do much to bring our professions together in a more complete understanding of the link between mind and body, which stands at the center of the healing arts.

—WALTER STEISS, M.D.

CONTENTS

III / LIFE CYCLES

IV / INFERENCES, BY-PRODUCTS, IMPLICATIONS

INTRODUCTION

EVERY THERAPIST LEADS A DOUBLE LIFE. TO HIS PATIENTS HE is a companion on the road from disillusion to strength—an interpreter, a guide, sometimes a friend, sometimes a friendly adversary, but always a companion. To the world in general, however, he is something quite different. He works as a detective, tracking down every aspect of human nature in search of some final understanding. Who are we? What makes us love, hate, care, deceive, or trust? Every case history he builds represents another set of clues to this central mystery. The therapist's responsibility is to record accurately his discoveries and to measure carefully his insights.

As a counseling psychologist setting down his findings in book form, I bear the weight of this responsibility; the burden is increased because I specialize in a relatively new and "unorthodox" technique, called Past Lives Therapy. It deals with reincarnation and thus with the flood of traumatic incidents that the unconscious mind seems capable of unleashing, dating back hundreds and sometimes thousands of years. I realize that I run the risk of offending many and leaving many others incredulous. But I hope that those who read *Past Lives Therapy* will consider the method on its merits, putting aside questions of paranormal phenomena long enough to comprehend the workings of the therapy itself. The curious, often baffling (to a nonbeliever) events that sometimes accompany the sessions between myself and my patients will be touched on throughout this book and dealt with in some detail toward the end. My primary aim, however, is to describe a therapeutic technique and, through the examination of case histories, to preserve a record of that technique at work. I am aware that many people find it difficult to accept any "scientific" therapy that deals with the question of past lives, and it is with this in mind that I offer these introductory notes.

People of the Western world tend to think of reincarnation in terms of the occult and the bizarre, but reincarnation is a part of the mainline philosophy practiced by nine hundred million Hindus, Buddhists, and Jainists. To these people the concept that we live more than once is as much a fact of life as Western religious beliefs are to us. They represent nearly a third of the world's population.

Past Lives Therapy treats reincarnation as a proven fact; it is, of course, nothing of the kind. I doubt very seriously whether reincarnation can ever be proven, and I really have no interest in proving it. We treat reincarnation as a reality because this is the only way for the therapy to function successfully. Patients recreate scenes in past lives for the purpose of understanding certain problems they have in the present; it would be pointless to question the veracity of the material they are reporting. Past Lives Therapy does not depend on the "truth" of reincarnation, but on putting aside the question of "truth" in order to work toward curing the patient's behavioral problem.

Having made this point, I must state my own belief at once, which is that reincarnation does in fact take place. I have been influenced in this belief by neither occultism nor Eastern religion, however. The belief has evolved by following my own observations to their logical conclusions. On the basis of the cases I have handled personally, and the independent research I have done, I feel that the theory of reincarnation *most logically* explains the phenomena I have witnessed.

Over the space of ten years I have had the same execution recounted to me in detail by eighteen separate patients who could not possibly have known each other. I have been able to verify such facts as dates of sea disasters and obscure suicides based on material given to me by patients with no expertise in these matters whatever. Since I am a psychologist, and not a professional researcher, I have not attempted to prove the truth of these events. Their use in the therapy is far more important to me than any "proof" that might be attained. Needless to say, the searching out of material that might validate these past lives is an intriguing pastime to many, and I have presented, in the final section of this book, several cases suggestive of reincarnation.

As far as my patients are concerned, the success of their therapy is unaffected whether they embrace a belief in reincarnation or remain skeptical throughout. Several people who have come to me claiming to be able to prove that reincarnation is a fraud have found themselves pushed to the wall by the revelations that they dig up about their own past lives. Others arrive at my office skeptical, work for three months, and depart equally skeptical. I take no position in all this. As a therapist my commitment is to my patients' psychological well-being. The technique I use is intended to serve their needs. In this book I merely record what I have found in my work and submit it to be judged by others.

I feel strongly that there are many aspects of our existence that we do not even begin to comprehend. We are just beginning to explore the link between mental distress and physical pain, disease, and deformity. Medicine has come a long way in treating the deterioration of the body, and psychology has made long strides in understanding the mind. But these two sciences have merely performed the preliminary functions. Understanding the link between the psychological and the physiological is the task at hand. Past Lives Therapy is a tentative step in this direction.

The evidence for reincarnation is certainly strong enough so that it can no longer be dismissed as a joke or a lunatic notion of some occult fringe. I have used it as a therapeutic tool for over a decade. Almost invariably my patients have found that their mental anguish in this life could be pinpointed to a physical situation in a past life. To put it in the simplest terms, a patient who suffers from an acute fear of heights, for example, will discover recurring past-life situations where he died by falling long distances. The past-life falls could easily be called "creative daydreams," and if a patient wishes to regard them that way I make no objection; the therapy will still work for him. As he detaches himself from the commands of past incarnations he loses the fear he has been suffering in the here and now. The notion that what he has been describing is, in fact, *real* is supported by the evidence he himself supplies concerning the time, place, conditions and language surrounding "past-life" incidents. We accumulate these details because it is essential for the patient to relive the trauma of each past-life incident moment by moment, fully and completely, in order to detach himself from it.

The notion of "detaching" a patient from his fears by making him relive them is not new. Freudian therapy has always involved patients in attempting to uncover their hidden trauma from very early life, and in World War II many shell-shock victims were cured of their disorientation by being forced to describe in detail and to emotionally relive their battlefield experiences. Unlike the victim of shell shock, however, my patient rarely knows the origin of his distress, and so we search together for the events he can recall that might have been the source of trauma. Really the only "unorthodox" aspect of my method is how far back I am willing to go to find that trauma: to the seeds of man's existence.

I have altered the following case histories only to protect the privacy of my patients. All the names used in this book are fictitious, and other minor details have been changed where it seemed that they might reveal a patient's identity. However, no substantive changes have been made in the information. The stories I have heard are presented as they evolved, reconstructed from extensive notes taken at each session. Many of them are not particularly pretty; trauma is caused by ugly, almost unendurable situations. The reader will find no mention in my cases of long, idyllic lives, brought to quiet and peaceful ends. This is not because no one has ever lived a happy past life, but because happy past lives create little turbulence in the unconscious mind. When a patient comes to me, we attempt to pinpoint his greatest pain, his most extreme difficulties in coping with life. Beginning with these emotions, he will scan the past to find their source. Naturally, he rarely comes upon happy times. If I were to begin my sessions by asking the patient to remember his most pleasurable emotions, he would undoubtedly come up with many pleasant periods in previous incarnations. But this would not be therapeutic counseling; it would be a mere parlor game involving reincarnation, worth neither the patient's time nor my own. Ultimately, such sessions would be anti-therapeutic. For just as negative behavior is controlled by past trauma that can be erased, positive behavior is the result of past fulfillment. It, too, can be erased. The results might include loss of productivity, security, and self-esteem for the participants.

People whose lives are untroubled by behavioral disorders would undoubtedly find a greater percentage of "happy" past lives than my patients do. They have no reason to explore these lives and would probably do best to leave the unconscious mind undisturbed. As for the material presented by my patients, its frequently brutal and tragic content is undeniable. It seems cowardly, however, to dress up or disguise it. I have no interest in creating any sort of sensational material; in fact, I have had nothing to do with the "creation" of these incidents. My job has been, simply, to guide my patients in finding the links between past and present and to help eliminate the past from a controlling position in their lives.

I

FINDING
PAST
LIVES

1

CONFRONTING
THE CRISIS

"I'VE TRIED EVERYTHING."

Alan Hassler stood just outside of my office door. He didn't say "Hello." He didn't say "Thank you for seeing me." He said "I've tried everything." The words came tumbling out as if he were delivering a prepared speech and had gotten through the first part of it before I'd opened the door. I had heard the phrase before, of course; I guess any psychologist hears it, but from Alan Hassler it represented a combative attitude I knew would be hard to overcome. Two weeks earlier he'd been a guest at my dinner table, and had listened carefully, like the good lawyer he is, as I explained the workings of Past Lives Therapy. We didn't know each other well (our wives were friends), but I could see that he was outraged by the thought of reincarnation and, despite our recent acquaintance, was not going to be polite about it. All conversation was brought to a halt while I was berated for my "misguided" work. Alan Hassler was certain that there was nothing after death and that my work consisted of selling "false hope" to unhappy wretches who didn't know any better. I declined to argue these points with my guest, because I knew that what I wanted to tell him would only feed his anger. I kept silent. Now, two weeks later, he was standing at my door, telling me he had tried everything. I was not particularly surprised. I told him to come in.

He sat nervously on the couch in my upstairs office. The self-confident bluster was gone. In a subtle way, the two weeks since I'd seen him had worn him out, slackened him. Somewhat overweight, he looked like a beaten man; his costly gray suit was rumpled, flecked with lint. In disorganized fragments, he gave me his background. He was a lawyer, with a good practice which he feared was collapsing, although it showed no signs of doing so. His first marriage had been, in his words, a "disaster"; now his second wife was threatening him with divorce.

"For the same reason," he told me. "Every time I see a domestic crisis coming, I just want to run and hide. I can go up against the toughest judge in the world and it's business as usual. But if my family has a problem I run out the back door. I can't help it. I just want to hide."

He had said it twice. I made a note of it and asked him about the marriage. His wife, it seemed, was a big spender. He was making a fair amount of money, but he felt she was working him to death. The fact that his perceptions of his homelife didn't really reflect what that life was like was a clear sign that he was reacting to a different situation, one which I suspected he would find in the past. Then the second phrase hit.

"I don't know what I'm working so hard for, it's hopeless." The past incident was coming into focus. I wrote down his second description—"it's hopeless"—and asked him to lie back and close his eyes.

I received a hard stare.

"You're here to work this out," I told him. "Otherwise you'd never have come to me."

He shrugged, reluctantly lay back on the couch, and closed his eyes.

"Take the phrase, 'I don't know what I'm working so hard for, it's hopeless.' "

"I dictated it into my dictaphone at the office," he admitted. "I threw away the belt."

"Repeat it again."

"I don't know why I'm working so hard. It's hopeless."

"Repeat, 'It's hopeless.' "

"It's hopeless."

"Again."

"It's hopeless."

"One more time, please."

"It's hopeless."

"Where do you go, what do you see, hear, think, feel?"

"Nothing."

He labored over this phrase for a few minutes, without saying anything further. I tried the phrase, "I want to hide," in the same manner, with the same results. Alan lay there, drawing a blank, repeating the phrase again and again. I could not accurately measure his reaction. Was he simply uncommitted to the work, or genuinely blocked? There was nothing on my pad except the two phrases he had given me. A blank spot suddenly filled itself in for me. I asked him to repeat the phrase he'd given me the moment he'd walked in the door.

"Take the phrase 'I've tried everything,' " I told him.

His body twitched. I saw his head cock slightly to the left, then he relaxed again. "I've tried everything—it's hopeless."

"What happened?" I asked.

"Nothing," he said, but I knew he was defending his problem. He had seen his incident for the first time, and lawyers hate to lose arguments.

"What's the next thing you hear, see, or feel?" I asked sternly.

There was a long pause. "I'm on a farm," he admitted. "On a farm, but it looks like a desert."

I began to make notes. "Repeat, 'I've tried everything.' "

"I *have* tried everything."

I knew he wasn't making the scene up, even if *he* wasn't sure yet. I now had to allow the incident to evolve.

"No rain," he said. "The climate has changed. I have been very successful, but the last year the crop was small. This year there is no crop."

"Next thing coming in—"

"My wife is going mad. She doesn't see that there is no way for us to go on living like we have in the past. She makes no sacrifices. They have taken away the house. We live in the barn. I've tried everything, but there's no rain. I've gone to town to sell the farm, but who would buy it?"

At this point Alan was still narrating, although the events were very real to him. Then, suddenly, his tone shifted. His breathing became heavier, his speech slower. He unleashed a flood of details.

"The wind is driving us crazy. The ground is just dust. It blows around the corners of the house, swirls up into the trees. I wear cloth around my head. I've worked so hard. It's hopeless."

Phrase number two. We repeated it four times. Little by little he came to see that this was the same phrase he used to describe his current life.

"The front yard is dust, swirling dust everywhere. No one would want to buy—"

In midphrase he stopped. His body froze in tension on the couch and the color drained from his face. Sweat beaded on his upper lip.

"Oh my God," he said quietly. "She's killed the children."

"Again."

"She's killed the children."

A pause of four or five seconds. Then the rest came rapidly, retarded only by my insistence that he repeat every salient phrase until his voice had lost its intensity.

"She's stabbed the children in the front yard. I have a pistol. The children are dead, drenched in blood, and I'm running. Running into the barn. She's there with the cloth around her head. I can't see her face, but she has a knife held to her own chest. I don't know what to do except with the pistol, and I fire it. She's thrown off her feet, covered with blood. Looking around. Nothing will grow."

I knew we had struck home, uncovered a scene that was crucially affecting Alan's view of "domestic crisis" in his current life. We went back to his discovery of the children and reworked it, gathering more details of the pain and revulsion —the blood on the bodies, the sudden nausea that swept over Alan as he viewed the scene, the sounds, and the feeling of the dust in his eyes. As we covered and recovered every step of this incident, Alan's emotional attachment gradually lost its muscle. Finally he was able to describe the scene with total calm and detachment. Only then did we move forward to the end of his life.

"I am taking the gun to my right temple. There's no hesitation as I pull the trigger. I'm glad to escape."

"Again."

"I'm glad to escape."

"Once more."

"I'm glad to escape."

As he described his own suicide, Alan Hassler kicked his head from right to left. The bullet entered the temple and lodged behind his eyes.

His first connection was made. I didn't ask Alan to believe that any of what he told me had actually happened. If he chose to think that it was the product of a suddenly unleashed imagination, his therapy could proceed at that level. After all, what a person makes up about himself is bound to reveal a lot about the person, his obsessions, fears, and self-image.

Alan Hassler, returned to a fully conscious state, wasn't sure where he had been. He admits to a rather limited imagination and is a poor storyteller. He agreed to place no immediate interpretation on the experience of coming in contact with a past-life incident. (Although he had reached a full, rich example of the kind of scene his unconscious mind associated with the notion of "domestic crisis," he was certainly not "cured.") During the next three months Alan and I explored many past incarnations. He stunned himself by discovering the subtle and curious links between his past experiences and his present life.

But it was this first swift, unexpected encounter that persuaded him to continue. Gradually, as the therapy produced results for him, his attitude toward it and toward reincarnation in general changed. It was not until he had seen the process work that I began to explain the full procedure and the scope of what I hoped we could accomplish together.

2

THE METHOD

THE WORKINGS OF PSYCHOTHERAPY SCARE A LOT OF PEOPLE; the process of bringing a patient from a point of despair to one of realistic hope seems magical—impossible to understand. Many like to believe it can't be done. But most methods of treatment are based on sound and simple principles, and Past Lives Therapy is no exception. It *is* a method of therapy. It *is not* in any way related to occultism, except that it shares an acceptance of the possibility of reincarnation.

Like many forms of psychotherapy, Past Lives Therapy assumes the existence of an unconscious mind. Freud and Jung discovered that our worst pain, our deepest fears, and our most affecting trauma are buried deep within us. We frequently cannot remember either the events that caused them, or the immediate results of those events. Only the scars are visible, in the form of behavioral problems. But the events have not disappeared from the memory; they are recorded in the unconscious mind. The Freudian analyst will reach back into the patient's earliest years to attempt to find the source of his current problems. Other therapists, such as Otto Rank, believed that the events of the patient's birth, and even the nine months in the womb prior to birth, were recorded in the unconscious. Past Lives Therapy simply takes the next step. We assume that the events of previous incarnations can have as devastating an effect on a patient's current behavior as anything that has happened to him in this life. Those events are as clearly recorded as are the events of this life, and they are just as accessible for use in therapy.

The unconscious mind operates like a tape recorder. Indiscriminately, it records and stores any and every event that takes place. While your conscious mind may refuse to acknowledge the more painful or terrifying events of your life, or "go into shock," the unconscious mind never shuts down. Its bank of information provides the conscious mind and emotions with a basis for the entire personality. When the unconscious mind is tapped, and begins to "play back," we find recall stretching far beyond the limits of this lifetime. The details of this recall make up the incidents a patient relives during a session of Past Lives Therapy.

Our first task in any session, of course, is to get the events exposed—to play back the incidents that the unconscious mind has recorded. Many psychologists have worked toward this end by using hypnotism and suggestion, but I find that this method handicaps the patient. He gives up a necessary control to the therapist, and is unable to take any positive action toward "erasing" the unconscious incident. It must always be the patient, and not the therapist, who does the work. To do so, he must be fully aware of what he is playing back, and how it affects him. My object, therefore, is to reach the unconscious without destroying the presence of the conscious. We begin with a simple observation on my part of the patient's frequently-used phrases.

THE PHRASES

Every man or woman uses the language in his own particular way. Each of us has phrases that seem to guide our lives. Not mottoes, not words of wisdom that we like to think of in stress situations, but commonplace phrases that seem to crop up in a recurring pattern in our daily conversation.

When a patient comes to me for therapy, I take a medical and family history, and discuss the patient's problems as he sees them. During this period I will be listening for specific recurring or out-of-place phrases. If a patient describes a constant state of anger, and puts it: "I'm burning up," or "I'm seeing red," I will take those phrases as literal descriptions of something in the patient's unconscious mind, something troubling, something trying to get out. Using these phrases as a guide, I will attempt to unlock the unconscious by asking the patient to lie down, close his eyes, concentrate on and repeat the phrases he has given me, until some kind of a mental picture or additional phrase emerges. At this point most patients fear that they will draw a blank—that they will "flop." But almost without exception the constant repetition of a phrase will jog the patient's mind to an image, and we will work forward from there. Frequently, when a new patient finally breaks through to his first past-life image, the scene will develop at a gallop, shocking the patient and almost overwhelming him. This was the case with Alan Hassler and his confrontation with domestic crisis. When a patient has difficulty contacting his first past-life incident, something is usually holding back his unconscious mind. He may have been blind, or deaf in the incident he wants to reach, or he may have unconsciously associated the incident with deep secrecy. There are methods for dealing with such "failures" in a patient's first session, but they are rarely needed. Usually, after a moment of hesitation, the unconscious mind unlocks itself. Frequently my most difficult task after that is to keep up with the barrage of incidents that are presented.

Throughout the process of revealing the past, the patient is fully aware of what is happening and can process the information that the unconscious mind is playing back. It is crucial that the patient understand the principles so that he can act upon them himself. In the casework section of this book I have condensed or eliminated the working dialogue between therapist and patient that reveals the mechanics of the session. To elucidate the process before examining specific behavioral problems, I present the following edited transcript of a session with a woman named Ann Boyd. The session took place six weeks into Ann's therapy.

THE SESSION

Ann Boyd was a tall, introverted woman of thirty-four. She was not unattractive, but her timidity made her unapproachable. In idle moments her eyes would lose focus as she lightly spun the hair near her ear between her thumb and index finger. Her presenting problem was her dealings with the opposite sex. It was impossible for her to establish a good relationship with a male. She had been married to an alcoholic for ten years, was recently divorced, and had gone through several subsequent relationships that had disintegrated quickly. She complained of pain during intercourse and overwhelming guilt at the end of each relationship.

"Men leave me, and I'm just crushed," she told me. "I feel like I'm being punished for my failure. I feel no man could possibly love me. It's futile."

From this small speech I made notes on my pad: painful sex, being crushed, being punished, futile love affair. These notes were the starting point for our session.

DR. NETHERTON: All right, lie down and close your eyes, and repeat the phrase "No man can possibly love me" again, again, and give me the first thing that comes to your mind.

ANN BOYD: I don't . . . "No man can possibly love me . . ."

DR. NETHERTON: Again.

ANN BOYD: "No man can possibly love me . . ." I can hear it.

DR. NETHERTON: When you hear that phrase, whom do you hear saying it? A male voice or a . . .

ANN: Female . . . I . . . where am I?

DR. NETHERTON: Indoors or outdoors? Give me the first answer you get!

ANN: *Outdoors.*

DR. NETHERTON: What do you see, hear, feel . . . ?

ANN: I'm frightened.

DR. NETHERTON: As if what is going to happen?

ANN: I'm falling.

DR. NETHERTON: As you fall, what's the next thing that comes to mind?

ANN: I'm pregnant. It's an earthquake, I'm falling into a hole. A long, long time ago.

DR. NETHERTON: What do you think, feel, see, hear?

ANN: I'm only fourteen, that priest made me pregnant. It's futile, I'll never have this baby.

DR. NETHERTON: Again.

ANN: It's futile, I'll never have this baby.

The phrase "it's futile" has controlled Ann's life up to this point. When we reach such a phrase in a past life, it is essential to erase it from the patient's unconscious. I have Ann repeat the phrase until she loses all emotional attachment to it and can see that it is a quote from the past, that it does not apply to the present. She must repeat the phrase until all the intensity drains from her voice. This usually happens within two or three repetitions. Each time we come upon the phrase "it's futile" in Ann's past (and there may be hundreds of occurrences), we must detach her from it. Little by little the effects of these erasures will be felt.

DR. NETHERTON: As you begin that fall, what are you feeling in your body? Let's feel the impact and the pain, and find what you are hearing, seeing, and thinking as it happens.

ANN: The earth is shaking all around me. The dirt's falling on top of me. I'm beginning to miscarry as I fall.

DR. NETHERTON: As you hit the ground, what part of your body hits first? Where do you feel that pain?

ANN: In my stomach. I'm going to lose my baby.

DR. NETHERTON: Next.

ANN: I hit the ground. It's hard. The dirt is falling in my face. It's crushing me.

DR. NETHERTON: Again.

ANN: It's crushing me.

DR. NETHERTON: Again.

ANN: It's crushing me.

DR. NETHERTON: What are you aware of now?

ANN: Weight on my chest. A stone is falling on my chest.

DR. NETHERTON: All right, as you feel that stone fall, tell me exactly what is happening.

ANN: I feel the impact. Now I'm feeling sharp pain. Something is sticking into my rib. It hurts. It hurts. It hurts.

We replay this scene in all of its detail, giving special attention to any physical pain, as many of Ann's current emotional problems are a throwback to incidents like the one she is describing. It is essential for her actually to *feel* the pain of the physical objects "crushing" her, so that she can detach herself from the emotional "crushing" she often describes in this life. Once she has fully experienced the pain of this earthquake situation she must detach herself and move on, leaving it behind forever.

ANN: Oh, my stomach hurts, my whole body hurts, but especially from right here on down. (She points to the area between the rib cage and the pelvis.) I've started cramping.

DR. NETHERTON: All right, where are the stones now?

ANN: On my face. Oh, my baby, my baby, my poor baby. I wish I could ease the pain for my baby.

DR. NETHERTON: Okay, what's the next thing that's happening?

ANN: I'm beginning to die now.

DR. NETHERTON: Okay, let that death happen. Move right through it.

ANN: I can't—I hurt.

DR. NETHERTON: What are you feeling?

ANN: The pain, I still hurt in my abdomen, and in my lower back.

When I find that a patient is unable to move into and through a death experience, I know that we have not totally erased the pain and trauma of the incident. Sometimes we have simply missed an important traumatic moment in the scene the patient is describing. More often the patient is attached to an earlier scene in the same lifetime and doesn't want to "die" without erasing the earlier experience. For this reason we frequently find ourselves jumping backward in time from the death scene to pick up early traumatic incidents. Such was the case with Ann.

DR. NETHERTON: Okay, let's become aware of how that pain got there. As you think of the two places where you hurt, what's happening in these places that is locking in the pain?

ANN: That man, when he raped me, it hurt me badly. He's a priest and everybody thinks he's a good man.

DR. NETHERTON: All right, move back to the rape. Let's see exactly what is happening.

ANN: He's knocking me down. He's holding a knife, right here. (She points to her chest.) I'm confused, I don't understand, I can't see anything.

DR. NETHERTON: Move through this and give me the next thing you're feeling.

ANN: I don't know, maybe God is punishing me?

DR. NETHERTON: Do you hear someone saying that?

ANN: Yes, she's saying, "God will punish you."

DR. NETHERTON: Again.

ANN: "God will punish you."

DR. NETHERTON: Who's saying that?

ANN: Somebody's watching.

DR. NETHERTON: Who?

ANN: A Sister. She's saying it to him. Oh, my God, my God, she's saying it to *him*!

At this point Ann began to shake uncontrollably, caught somewhere between laughter and tears. For years she'd been living under a cloud of guilt caused by the unconscious command: God will punish you. The fact that the words had never been directed at her, but at her attacker, was a revelation. In the rape situation Ann (whatever her name was in that life) was in shock, her conscious mind at a dead halt, and the entire incident was recorded word for word in her unconscious mind. For her whole life she has vaguely felt that she would be punished, that she *should* be punished. The sudden revelation was almost too much for her. We repeated this incident several times, after which I saw a different person lying on the couch. Muscle tensions that had lined her face since I had known her were gone. Her eyes, which had always seemed to be looking for a place to hide, were clear and in repose. She picked up the thread of the rape easily.

ANN: He doesn't care that she's saying it to him. I'm very confused. My head is hit, oh, he's inside me now . . . he's moving. . . . I don't feel very much . . . dry . . . numb. . . . Then he puts it in my mouth . . .

DR. NETHERTON: Let the unconscious move through the experience, keep moving through it.

ANN: I'll show you, I'll show you . . . I'll show you: I don't like the taste or the smell . . . I'm choking . . .

DR. NETHERTON: Move right on through and past it. . . . What's the next thing coming in now?

ANN: He hits my behind, stands me up, says, "Now get out of here."

DR. NETHERTON: What's coming in next?

ANN: I'm crouching outside a building waiting for my opportunity to get away . . . this is different, though. It's later . . . I know I'm pregnant. . . . The earth begins to break. I feel God is punishing me, I'm ruined. . . . No man can possibly love me.

DR. NETHERTON: Repeat.

ANN: No man can possibly love me.

DR. NETHERTON: Again.

ANN: No man can possibly love me. . . . Now's my chance to run free . . . I'm running, running through a grassy field, it smells wonderful, I love the smell of pollen, fresh-cut grass, it's my favorite smell ever, it is freedom, the sky is so blue, but it's cracking open, into pieces, the earth is cracking open all around me, I'm running, running into the wind, breathless, there's a cornfield in front of me, it's pretty, golden . . .

DR. NETHERTON: The earth—

ANN: It's cracking, I have the sensation of falling, wherever I put my feet down, I'm afraid of falling, I feel peace, I know I'm going to die soon. I'm falling into the hole now.

Here we've returned to the death scene, having hopefully cleared out any trauma preventing Ann from leaving this past life. But there is more here we must work.

DR. NETHERTON: All right, as you are falling into the hole this time, are you attached to any of those things we first worked?

ANN: The dirt in my face.

DR. NETHERTON: Where's the dirt now?

ANN: In my mouth. Ugh! It's like manure. It's disgusting.

DR. NETHERTON: All right, what's happening now?

ANN: I'm in the hole, the stones are all around. . . .

DR. NETHERTON: Okay, and the next . . . ?

ANN: I'm listening.

DR. NETHERTON: What are you hearing?

ANN: My mother.

DR. NETHERTON: What's she saying?

ANN: He'll never love you now.

DR. NETHERTON: Again.

ANN: He'll never love you now.

DR. NETHERTON: One more time.

ANN: He'll never love you now.

Once again we must move backward and play out a prior scene in this lifetime. This kind of back-and-forth chronology is common in Past Lives work; the unconscious mind seems to release incidents in illogical sequence, one triggering another like a gang of fireworks on a single fuse. A momentary image or phrase in one scene will bring an entirely different scene into focus. It is essential for the therapist to play out each scene as it comes up. I will leave Ann's death scene as many times as she finds places to take me, always returning, finally, to the ultimate pain and trauma of death. When we have moved through the death, we will rework the entire lifetime, putting it in chronological order and scanning it for any further incidents she may find.

DR. NETHERTON: What's the next thing evolving in there?

ANN: There's a boy who said he'd marry me.

DR. NETHERTON: Again.

ANN: There's a boy who said he'd marry me. He's my friend. We've walked and talked together. He's the only person I've told that I'm trying to learn to read and write. My mother told me I shouldn't learn to read and write. . . .

My mother's saying . . . "He'll never marry you now, you're ruined. . . ."

DR. NETHERTON: Good. Is this before or after the rape incident?

ANN: After.

DR. NETHERTON: Good. What's the next thing coming in?

ANN: The dirt—in my mouth. I'm in the hole. This is all happening very quickly. I don't feel very much. I'm sad, but there's not too much pain. I'm . . . maybe I'm in shock.

DR. NETHERTON: What are you feeling?

ANN: I'm sad about the baby. I wanted to grow up and have a man take me away.

DR. NETHERTON: Again.

ANN: I wanted to grow up and have a man take me away. I wanted to have a baby later . . . not now. Still, we're dying together. I can feel the weight. I'm not even struggling to get out of the dirt. I know it's futile.

DR. NETHERTON: Again.

ANN: I know it's futile.

DR. NETHERTON: Again.

ANN: I know it's futile. I'm dying now. I've given up. The pain has stopped. I don't know what's happened.

DR. NETHERTON: Are you dead?

ANN: I think I am. I'm not there anymore. . . .

DR. NETHERTON: Good, all right, let's just scan this entire incident. Can you look at it all?

ANN: Yes.

DR. NETHERTON: Have we got it all in order now so that you have no attachment for it?

ANN: Yes.

DR. NETHERTON: Okay, let the unconscious mind move where it wants to now, let's see where the reinforcements for these patterns come in.

ANN: I'm being hanged. I'm blindfolded, but somehow I can see, at least . . . I know what's happening. . . . I think I'm blinded, maybe I was blinded earlier . . . there's a fire about to be lit. . . .

Here, Ann has encountered another life, a life where she will see many of the same patterns, though the circumstances are different.

DR. NETHERTON: Let's have the first word or thought that comes to mind.

ANN: It's hopeless.

DR. NETHERTON: Are you thinking or is someone saying it?

ANN: I see a young boy, he was supposed to marry me . . . he's betraying me. I want to cry and I can't, I think if I could just cry before I die I'd feel better. . . . I can't, I'm choking . . . I'm choking on my own tears . . .

DR. NETHERTON: Okay, let's move right on through it . . . what are you feeling?

ANN: The rope around my neck hurts.

DR. NETHERTON: Describe it—

ANN: Rough, I never realized the skin on my neck was so tender, so soft. . . . Pain in my chest . . . the rope tightened . . . I'm hearing a lot of yelling now . . .

DR. NETHERTON: The exact words . . .

ANN: "God will punish you . . . God will punish you . . . God will punish you!"

DR. NETHERTON: And the next . . .

ANN: They have a book, a book that tells about witches . . . it's black . . . they look at the book and say that I'm a witch . . .

DR. NETHERTON: Move right on . . .

ANN: There's a man . . . that young man I see in the crowd. . . . I can see slightly. He kissed me . . . said he would come back and take me to marry him. . . . I told my mother and she said he'd never have the courage to do that. . . . He'll marry the woman he's supposed to marry. . . . His fiancée sends these men to get me, she says I'm a witch . . .

DR. NETHERTON: Where are you when they come to get you?

ANN: I'm a tamer of wild beasts . . . the animals eat out of my hand . . . there's a wolf who follows me everywhere . . . they all like me . . .

DR. NETHERTON: What's happening with this man and his fiancée?

ANN: He told her he wants to marry me. . . . She accuses me of making a potion to steal the man's love. The men believe her, not me . . . they take me away. . . . This is in Germany . . . the Black Forest region . . . *Wälder* . . . it's the German word for forests. . . . I see a bay . . .

DR. NETHERTON: What's happening now?

ANN: We're at a little shed . . . they're tying my hands behind my back . . . they're pulling the rope tighter . . . they've lit the fire . . .

DR. NETHERTON: Move right on through it now.

ANN: My ribs are broken from a rope pulled tight, they're pulling it tighter . . . it's crushing me, crushing my ribs.

DR. NETHERTON: Let's feel the damage being done . . .

ANN: Damage to my lungs . . . I'm crushed.

DR. NETHERTON: Again.

ANN: I'm crushed.

DR. NETHERTON: Once more.

ANN: I'm crushed.

DR. NETHERTON: What are you feeling next?

ANN: Hopeless. He'll never love me . . . I'll never be able to live like a normal woman . . .

DR. NETHERTON: Next thing you're aware of . . .

ANN: I'm afraid. I'm burning . . . I hope they break my neck first so I don't have to feel it. . . . I can feel the heat . . . I start screaming . . . I have to get out of here. I can't stand it. . . . The fire comes up all around me.

DR. NETHERTON: What are you feeling now?

ANN: Not too much, I'm pretty preoccupied with the burning. . . . I'm finally dying . . . I feel relieved . . .

DR. NETHERTON: If you were screaming out loud, what words would we hear?

ANN: None. I'm dying. I'm leaving the body, I'm aware of leaving . . . of going out of it . . . I want to rest very badly . . .

DR. NETHERTON: As you leave that body where you've been burned and hanged are you taking anything with you?

ANN: Something—while I'm burning, I'm still angry with the man who was supposed to marry me. . . . He left me at such a crucial time.

DR. NETHERTON: Notice how you replay that. The men you are involved with in *this* life all leave you at crucial times. All right, are you out of that body now with no attachments?

ANN: Yes.

DR. NETHERTON: All right. Give me the next thing evolving in there. What's the first thing you pick up?

ANN: She's sad.

DR. NETHERTON: Again.

ANN: She's sad. It's my mother. Just lying in bed, but she can't get comfortable.

Here Ann has hit upon an incident taking place in the prenatal period of her current lifetime. This is an essential part of her session. The past lives that each patient relives seem to have common themes—in Ann's case recurring scenes of being crushed, and recurring betrayals by men. The choice of which themes will govern a patient's life is made during the prenatal period, birth, and early childhood of this life. Ann quite possibly has lived a series of untroubled lives, and undergone many natural, relatively painless deaths, but if nothing in her prenatal period, birth, or early childhood restimulates these lives, she will never be influenced by them, or recall them.

No past-life incident is completely erased until we find the prenatal, birth, or childhood incident in the present life that restimulated it. For this reason almost every session concludes with a search of these areas.

DR. NETHERTON: Quote me exactly what you are hearing. If she were talking out loud, what would we hear?

ANN: She's on her back, but there's a great weight from the baby. She feels she's being crushed, and she's turning on her side.

DR. NETHERTON: What's she thinking now?

ANN: "I'm pregnant—how futile! It's by a man I don't love, we're both big and clumsy, and the baby will be, too.

No one will ever love her."
DR. NETHERTON: Repeat.
ANN: "No one will ever love her."
DR. NETHERTON: Okay. The next thing coming in.
ANN: Tightness. A squeezing around my ribs. It's that crushing again. The same crushing. A voice saying "big beautiful eyes," but all I feel is this pressure. I can't breathe. It's easing now, but I'm frightened. It's easing now. It's very bright. I'm frightened. This is the delivery room. I've just arrived.
DR. NETHERTON: All right. Do you see any attachments now to anything we've worked on? Do you see, hear, or feel anything that will keep you attached to these incidents?
ANN: No.
DR. NETHERTON: Okay. And what are you feeling now?
ANN: Very calm. Very . . . (here she opens her eyes). I feel fine. Very composed.

At this point Ann is once again fully in the present. Her unconscious mind has receded. The session is complete. To conclude the appointment, I may discuss with a patient like Ann the connections between her prenatal or birth incidents and the past-life incidents she has relived. In the session above, Ann had been in therapy long enough so that she could make the associations by herself.

When a fetus is developing, it is controlled completely by the emotions of the mother carrying it. It takes the mother's feelings as its own. Ann's mother thinking that she's being crushed by the weight of the developing fetus amounts to the same thing as the fetus itself thinking it's being crushed. This incident triggered the scene of being buried alive, as did the passage through the birth canal, where the baby felt an overwhelming sensation of being crushed by the vaginal wall.

The restimulation of the rape by a priest is somewhat harder to follow without a complete understanding of the importance of phrases. In the past life, Ann's mother had reacted to her rape by saying (about a fiancé), "He'll *never* love you now." That phrase focused the trauma of the rape for Ann. In the prenatal period of her present life her present mother thought "no one will *ever* love her." The matching of the two phrases, both said by mothers, both carrying the same traumatic implication, both made up of similar words, restimulated the rape incident. In her current life the rape was being unconsciously replayed every time she had intercourse, causing pain, frustration, and further guilt.

Every new relationship Ann undertook immediately triggered this tangle of hopelessness and despair. Her constantly repeated phrase, "it's futile," had become a self-fulfilling prophecy.

Within a remarkably short period the futility began to evaporate. The following week Ann arrived early at my office. The change that had come over her reminded me of the scenes in romantic Hollywood movies where mousy girls remove their glasses and suddenly bloom into raving beauties. Her walk was more confident and her clothes were brighter, her speech patterns were freer and her smile wider. I knew why: With the rape pattern gone, she had enjoyed a sexual relationship for the first time in her life. The change was highly dramatic, but not yet complete. Although she no longer felt pain during the sex act, Ann had much work to do in improving her self-esteem. Past Lives Therapy is a very "problem-oriented" technique. We take each symptom and work with it specifically. No session results in a patient suddenly becoming a perfectly balanced individual; rather we achieve balance by chipping away at the patient's problems one by one. As each one drops away we gain a step toward security and health.

THE METHOD

One can observe from the above transcription that there are four crucial elements operating in any Past Lives Therapy session; these four are the backbone of the method. The first is the request for data from the unconscious mind, while the conscious mind stays present. The fact that the unconscious communicates voluntarily, and not by hypnotic inducement, allows the patient to see clearly where he is as he is reliving the experiences. Secondly, the careful reconstruction of pain and emotional trauma is vital. I will gather information about a patient's death detail by detail, and the patient must actively go through each death. Each incident must be run out of the unconscious exactly as it was put in. It is only by feeling the agony that one can detach oneself from it.

Eventually, as a patient relives the trauma, he will use the phrase that originally triggered recall of the incident—the phrase we began the session with. He may find several variants of this phrase. Each time he uses it, I will have him repeat it until he separates himself from the trauma associated with it. This repetition and detachment process is the third step. The repetition of a phrase, such as "it's hopeless," brings the patient to a focus on how the past affects the present. The first time the phrase is said, the patient is barely aware of the connection between past and present. The second time he feels the emotion generated by the phrase. By the third repetition, the voice is neutral, emotionless, and a sense of perspective prevails.

At the end of the session we search the prenatal period, birth experience, and childhood for events and phrases that triggered the pertinent past-life experiences. This is the fourth and final element.

The topic of each session is determined by whatever problem the patient presents when he arrives at my office. Inevitably the problem, when explored, brings us back to the same patterns we find in childhood, stretching back through the birth experience into the prenatal period. The average session lasts from two to two-and-a-half hours. The length of therapy is usually three months of weekly sessions. Some patients return from time to time after that, but no one is with me in therapy for years and years or on a daily basis.

My work deals with the entire range of human behavioral problems, from sexual inadequacies and serious phobias to problems that may seem minor to some, such as chronic common colds, migraines, and stuttering. I have dealt with problems outside the range of normal psychological care, such as cancer (see Chapter 12) and epilepsy (see Chapter 5), and have had success with both.

By exploring many of the above cases in detail I hope to bring the therapy further into focus, and also to offer some insight into the nature of the disorders themselves. The reader will find that Past Lives Therapy is not a miracle cure, nor am I a "healer" in any sense of the word. The patient is responsible for his own improvement. He can, with a substantial amount of work and concentration, put the past behind him and keep it from intruding on the present, allowing the full force of his human potential to be realized.

II

CASEWORK

A NOTE ON THE CASEWORK

IT IS MY BELIEF THAT, AT SOME LEVEL, ALL DISEASE BEGINS with the mind. This section of case histories is organized to focus on that assertion. It begins with an examination of claustrophobia, a disorder normally thought to be "purely mental," and concludes with a case of incipient cervical cancer, a disease that most doctors would argue is wholly physiological. In moving from one extreme to the other, I have tried to show the ways in which the unconscious mind commands the body to malfunction.

In some chapters of this section I have moved the contents of several sessions' work into immediate juxtaposition to clarify a given problem for the reader. Each case represents the incidents from many sessions. If I sometimes give the impression that a patient's condition disappeared after one or two sessions, it is because of this juxtaposition and not because Past Lives Therapy is able to work miracles. For the most part the cases in this section represent between two and three months' work each.

3

CLAUSTROPHOBIA

COREY HOPKINS

THE AVERAGE MAN OR WOMAN SUFFERS FROM A BATTERY OF
minor fears. I would guess that no one is entirely free of
them. For the most part they do not disturb our existence,
although they may be a slight inconvenience. People experience a distaste for using the telephone, for clothes shopping,
for driving, or for other necessary activities. In slightly more
serious cases we find people who will not eat certain foods
or will not wait in crowded places. We live with these phobias because they are less trouble to tolerate than to deal
with. Some people, however, experience fear in the extreme
and begin to exhibit actual signs of panic when placed in a
crowd or forced to look down from great heights. Often they
must readjust their lives drastically to accommodate their
fears. The businessman who will not have a meeting above
the fourth floor of a building, the housewife who will not go
out at all for fear of being trapped in a crowded bus—these
people are living truly disrupted lives. Frequently they come
to therapists for help.

They tend to be totally bewildered. Unlike the ulcer or
migraine sufferer, who usually senses that his problem is tied
to extreme nervousness or pressure, the phobia patient has
no idea why he or she is so susceptible to panic. Nothing in
this life seems to be causing the problem. For these patients,
Past Lives Therapy can be extremely effective.

Claustrophobia is usually thought of as a morbid dread of
being stuck in a small, narrow, or confined space. The sufferer usually presents a broad range of symptoms, however.

When Corey Hopkins first made an appointment to see me, she described her condition as a constant state of "being shoved and bumped," "unable to get my breath," and "stuck in a mess." She never mentioned specifically tight, confined, or narrow spaces, but as she described her daily life, it became clear that she was living in fear of being trapped; even in the open outdoors she frequently experienced a sense of panic about "the walls closing in."

She was twenty-four years old, with a highly angular face and a wide mouth. She had a spontaneous, almost rebellious personality that should have been attractive to men, but her romantic life was unsatisfactory. She expressed an almost obsessive embarrassment about the size of her hips and thighs, which were a few pounds heavier than they might have been but were certainly within the normal range. She could not be convinced of this, however, and felt that her embarrassment was hurting her social life. During her initial interview she spoke of being "wrapped in fat" and "pulled down by [her] fat thighs."

Corey was the daughter of an alcoholic father and a conservative, highly religious mother; she felt hemmed in by both of them. Tension in the family had increased to the breaking point as the result of a relationship Corey had begun with a black Vietnam War veteran. She herself was unable to explain the relationship, claiming that the man frequently threatened her with violence and seemed to be using her, primarily to shore up his own flagging sense of authority. Despite the feeling that she was being treated "like a piece of property," Corey could not seem to give this man up and was considering marriage. Her submissive behavior fulfilled her in some disturbed way, and this led to great distress.

The company Corey worked for had gone out of business and she had been involved in the cleanup operation. As she described the dismantling of what had been a complex operation, I began to get a sense of the delicacy of her condition. In the transcriptions below, I have eliminated my routine questions, and put Corey's answers in paragraph form. This is done as a convenience to the reader, and nothing of importance has been eliminated.

. . . It was an awful mess. I looked around at all the papers and boxes and files, and I really began to just shake. I thought, "My God, it'll never be right again, I'll never get things in order. I felt like I was just being pushed around by the mess. A few times I had to leave the room, for walks, and even then I found myself holding my breath until I nearly passed out. I just couldn't take hold of myself.

I asked Corey to lie down and let the feeling of being pushed around, and the panic of not having any breath, run through her mind. I repeated the feelings she had described to me several times.

"If you're being jostled, pushed, if you're gasping for breath, where are you? Do you hear voices? A phrase, a word?"

A quizzical look crossed Corey's face as she said the phrase, "Well, this is my house. I guess I'll just have to live here."

The phrase came out of nowhere and made no particular sense, in the context of our conversation. I knew Corey had found something that we could build on, but I didn't know what.

"Who's saying that?" I asked.

"I . . . no one's saying it, I think I'm thinking it. . . . A man has me. By the shoulders. It's him. It's him. He's saying . . . 'This'll be your house, you'll just get used to it.' "

"Where are you?"

I'm looking at a big . . . crate. Not as tall as I am and . . . Oh my God, that's what he's talking about. This big crate. I'm going to have to *live* in it. He's opening the door and pushing, and I fall inside. He slams the door on me, and I can hear him walking away. . . . "Have fun." He's saying it so cool, like it . . . doesn't mean a thing to him.

Corey described the crate's shape clearly but couldn't say anything about the rest of its appearance, since she was in total darkness. Her attempts to break out were futile.

I begin to scream, and beat my fists, but I'm all alone, I guess. I slump down in a corner, curled up—there's no way to stretch out the length of my body in here, not in any direction. I curl around myself in a corner, just whimpering. Hours and hours, and finally a crack of light. . . . I leap up and begin banging, but it's the sun. The sun is coming up. I don't know how long this is going on. I'm banging and slumping down and getting up and banging again. I can't rest, it's just . . . my limbs are shaking. It's panic.

At length, Corey recalled, someone brought her a muffin and a cup of water and pulled her out of the crate, where she had evidently spent the night. A large, uniformed man took her and a group of other women into a circular public shower. It was here that we finally came upon Corey's true circumstance.

I'm . . . black, I'm black. With a brand on my left shoulder. They're marching us around and around this room, spraying us from nozzles and there are . . . seven, I think seven corridors leading into this room—spokes of a wheel. More and more women are piling in, but it feels good to walk. I'm stretching at last, and I feel like I could walk forever. I'm . . . a slave, but I don't know where . . . I was sold to a man for domestic service, but all he wanted to do was . . . use me sexually . . . rape me. He chased me around, but I wouldn't do it, and now I'm here. I don't know why, maybe I was sold back? There are a lot of us now, and I slow down the walk. I guess they're exercising us, but it's too crowded; women are streaming in from the corridors, and I can't move.

As Corey described the crowd assembling around her in the bathhouse she began to wrench around uncomfortably on my couch, exhibiting the signs of approaching panic. Her back arched suddenly, and her involvement with the past experience was total.

"What's happening?" I asked.

This girl stepped on my foot and I pushed her. I'm saying, "Goddamn you, leave me alone, get away from me!" Now they're fighting, there's a mclee breaking out, we're all swinging, and the men are laughing, watching, but I don't know what to do. I'm just trying to get out. There's all these bodies and I'm in the middle. I'm just trying to pull myself out and over, but I'm being dragged down from the bottom . . . someone . . . everyone's closing in around my legs and pulling me down—grabbing me around the waist.

This last statement, which seems simple enough, and without significance, is the kind of clue that a trained Past Lives therapist will single out from the rest of the scene. Corey's inappropriate fears about the weight of her thighs and hips had seemed somehow tied to her claustrophobic panic, and this was the link—a panic in a past life caused by her being dragged down into a crowd by the waist, hips, and thighs. She continues:

The men have had their fun, now they're cracking whips to herd us into line. We're looking around as they shout, and then there's quiet. The woman I pushed is pointing at me and shouting "She did it! She did it!" and two men grab me. Someone behind me, very quiet, a man, says, "Put her in the hot box." Oh God, not again, not again.

Corey was placed back in the crate for an undeterminable period of time. She recalled the light coming and going as the days went by. Before long she was forced to relieve herself in her tiny cubicle. Living in her own filth was unbearable. She would attempt to hold her breath for long periods of time, finally having to gasp for the fetid, repulsive air around her in order to survive. Once again we came upon a contemporary symptom. When describing the cleaning of her "messy" office, Corey had found it difficult to breathe. All of

Corey's phobic reactions to performing what most people would consider a normal task were tied to experiences such as the one she was describing. The ending of her slave life proved to be a classic claustrophobic nightmare:

> They've put us on a boat . . . hundreds of us down in the hold, that same awful stench and the moaning and dark . . . dark, day and night. Then there's a light from above, it's blinding . . . it's probably not all that light, but I haven't seen any for so long . . . and a man's screaming, "Get them up! Get them out!" I don't know what's happening, but there's this huge cracking sound, like an explosion, but it's wood cracking. The water starts to rush up from below, my God, the water, we're just squirming around, desperate. . . . I have no control, I can't move my arms or legs . . . it's awful . . . out of control and the water is just rising, I can see it . . . that's all there will be for me. It's burning my lungs, a burning feeling, not like it's wet at all, just searing, and I'm gone. Gone.

"Are you leaving your body?" I asked Corey.

"Yes," she said. "I'm not there anymore. All that wreckage, it just floats below me."

"Where are you now?"

"In a . . . hut. A hot climate . . . years ago, I don't see anything I recognize. . . . These must be very primitive people."

Corey described a life which, in all likelihood, took place before her life as a slave. She remembered nothing about the life but the end of it. As she sat in her hut, resenting the absence of her husband and son, who were off hunting, an earthquake struck the area, and Corey leapt forward out of the collapsing structure.

> But the ground is breaking and it's . . . got me. I'm sinking and the dirt is rolling over on itself, driving me down, pulling me down as I kick and climb. I'm pulling so hard . . . and sinking! It's all around me, up over my head, and in my face . . . I'll never breathe, never. . . .

I can't . . . take a breath. I'm gasping . . . I'm gasping . . . getting dirt. No air.

Again we replayed a scene where Corey found suffocating panic the controlling emotion of a death incident. The attempted escape from a collapsing structure (like her office) led to a fatal dragging down from the thighs and hips.

This incident confirmed the claustrophobic pattern—the continual threat of unexpected confinement, especially centered in the hips and thighs. A very minor part of Corey's description proved to be the starting point for the second phase of her therapy. She had stated that moments before the earthquake her strongest emotion was resentment toward her mate. He had gone hunting and left her alone. Although she did not say so, she was obeying his will by staying home. In her slave life she had been at the mercy of a group of men who determined when she would be punished and when she could walk free. In beginning a session with Corey's feelings toward her dominating boyfriend, we found important reinforcements for this sense of being controlled by men. Corey relived an incident in France in which she worked as a prostitute for a pimp/lover who supplied her with heroin but never paid her. A mysterious image that recurred through this session was a swirling impression of a hand-cranked carrousel with a calliope playing in the background, and Corey riding around and around while her procurer pricked her arm with a crude needle and then applied the mouth of a leather pouch of heroin to the open vein. There was a delirious thrill about the scene, a kind of ecstasy that explained why she sometimes felt content to be with this man, whom she knew was using her. These sessions slowly progressed, and Corey lost her dependence on her current relationship and the feelings of worthlessness that went with it.

Through careful working and repetition Corey became completely detached from this artificially induced euphoria. She realized that she unconsciously associated her submissive tendencies with a kind of perverse, short-lived happiness. In breaking this attachment, Corey would, I knew, be putting her current relationship in jeopardy, and it would not last long. Although she went through a painful breakup period, the results were a vastly improved sense of self-worth, and a freedom to accept more valuable relationships.

The prenatal period of Corey's present life revealed her mother's constant worry that the family house would be too small to accommodate another child. Although this subject may have masked much deeper worries about adding a newborn to the family, Mrs. Hopkins seemed to be concentrating on it as the cause for all of her unhappiness. Corey recalled her lying on a living-room couch throughout the pregnancy, worn out by the summer heat, barely moving.

"There's no room for it," was the constant thought. "The house is too tiny, it's always a mess if one thing gets out of place. The minute it gets overcrowded everything will go to hell, I won't be able to keep it up. It looks like an earthquake hit around here most of the time anyhow."

Evidently there was construction around the house during the last months of pregnancy, and the noise made it impossible for Corey's mother to rest properly. She would lie with her hands over her ears, thinking, "I'm going crazy here. I've got to get out. I've got to leave now."

These feelings dominated the development of the fetus. The nine months of gestation were spent in an atmosphere of ever-increasing oppressiveness, as the heat, the noise, and the mother's own unwillingness to welcome the expected baby battled each other for attention.

Corey's most vivid recollections were of her own delivery. Because the obstetrician had become involved in an emergency delivery and was late in attending Corey's mother, nurses watching the patient coaxed her to "hold on," to "not let go until Doctor arrives."

Here the two major themes of Corey's therapy converge. At the moment before her entrance into this world, the actions of a man, the doctor, control the claustrophobic situation. Held against her will in the womb, awaiting the man who will release her, Corey's unconscious plays back every previous occasion where she was kept in the same bind. The pressure, the sense of waiting for escape, becomes overwhelming. At one point Corey's mother's vagina was packed in ice to slow the delivery, and two nurses held her legs together. All of this was released with the arrival of the doctor, and the birth itself was normal.

Unfortunately, the damage had been done. Corey's delivery scene had triggered the hot-box panic, the drowning in a sea of humanity and water, the fear of a "messy" existence surrounded by her own waste products, and the dread of being buried alive by earthquake. These were the incidents that dominated her life.

We returned to this delivery scene in nearly every session, working different aspects of it each time. The cumulative effect was substantial. Corey began to adjust more easily to her surroundings and realized that she was no longer gasping for air, even in difficult or trying situations. Her near-engagement to the dominating boyfriend ended with a good deal of pain, but Corey dealt with that unhappiness in a rational way and it did not seem to induce attacks of the claustrophobic panic that it once would have. Although still unhappy about the weight of her hips, Corey paid less and less attention to the problem once she saw that it was not affecting her social life in any way. I offered to explore the issue of her weight in a third phase of therapy, but Corey felt, much to my satisfaction, that the problem was too trivial. At that point she was happily out of my hands.

4

ULCERS

CARL PARSONS

THE LINK BETWEEN EMOTIONAL STRESS AND PHYSICAL DISEASE
has defied human understanding for centuries. Our knowledge of this subject is slight and uncertain. The suggestion
that people with certain emotional patterns are prone to get
diseases such as arthritis and cancer is greeted with immediate disbelief in most circles; the great exception to this
blanket skepticism is the ulcer. Everyone seems willing to
acknowledge the existence of an "ulcer personality." I believe
that the coming years will produce overwhelming evidence
that there is a "cancer personality," an "arthritis personality,"
possibly even a "common cold personality." In later chapters
I will describe a cancer patient and an epileptic, both of
whom improved radically when we explored the emotional
components of their diseases. I choose to begin with the case
of ulcers simply because the link between the "worrier" and
his physically disabled stomach is one that is widely accepted.

Carl Parsons was tall, stoop shouldered, and sallow. He
was in his mid-thirties when he came to me for treatment,
but his flesh showed the slackening of a much older man.
As he gave me his medical and personal history his foot beat
a soft, rapid tattoo against my desk leg; his right thumb and
index finger constantly slid his wedding ring up and down
his left ring finger. These nervous habits were coupled with
a jarring stop-and-start speech pattern—short bursts of words
and long pauses.

Carl was in charge of a failing electronics/engineering
firm. He was a typical "ulcer personality." Obsessed with the

idea that he would "lose everything," he had experienced pain just below the solar plexus for some months, along with serious loss of sleep, constant indigestion, and resultant loss of weight. In addition, he suffered frequent impotence, which is an unusual symptom for an ulcer patient. His doctor reported no serious damage to the stomach yet, but felt it was only a matter of time before an actual ulcer developed. His stomach lining showed some irritation, and I was not sure what could be done about that. (I would never claim that therapy of this kind can regenerate damaged tissue or repair any other physical destruction in the body.)

I was interested in Carl's impotence, first because it was the least common symptom of the ulcer-prone patient, and secondly because it was obviously contributing to his overall unhappiness, and might, I felt, be an actual *cause* of his problem, rather than a *result* of it. As it turned out, I was wrong, but the sexual difficulty played into the past-life spectrum in an interesting way nonetheless.

I asked Carl to tell me what it was like, this pain in the gut he felt almost daily.

"It feels like a hot poker being run right through me," he said.

This phrase began our session.

"Now, if someone were running a hot poker through you, what would be your first feeling or awareness?"

"Words like 'You son of a bitch!' But those aren't the actual words. . . . I hear a sound, a . . . voice speaking something but . . . it isn't 'you son of a bitch,' but that's what it means, more or less."

We had struck something, probably a scene where no language like our own was spoken, and I asked Carl about the setting, about the feeling of the place where he found himself. He began to describe a village with thatched huts, possibly somewhere in Africa or South America, a hot climate, in very primitive times.

I had been trying to win this girl, a thirteen- or fourteen-year-old girl . . . for a wife, but my . . . rival, my sworn enemy, he took her instead. The tribal fathers decided. He took her and they have a hut near mine. I hear them moaning in the night, whining and insulting me with their . . . noise. But now he's off . . . to the hunt? To a war? I really don't know. He's not there and I've lifted up the flap to the door and she's in there. . . . We don't wear any clothes, I guess, at least we don't wear any at the moment. She's not . . . I guess she doesn't know how to object . . . women just don't here. I'm, uh, mounting her and we're rocking back and forth on some skins on the floor. But now . . . the light! Someone's opened the door—the flap—and I'm being pulled off. He's come back! With his spear, his hunting spear. He is shouting, "You son of a bitch!" in the . . . it's a different language but that's the exact phrase! "You son of a bitch, you'll never make love to another man's woman!" And he . . . he pushes me across the room. He hurls the spear right—!

At this point Carl twitched back toward the wall from the couch he was on, and grabbed himself across the solar plexus. He was feeling the pain he felt every day, but now he had a new explanation for it.

He's got me, right here in the gut, right here, and I'm . . . it went right through and I'm pinned to a post holding up the hut. Now he's reaching down and, oh my God, he's cutting it off. My penis, he's . . . but I can't feel it, I'm . . . I guess it's shock. Oh, I'm paralyzed. The pain is all in the gut. I can't feel anything below. I'm slumping now and I can't feel, I . . . I guess . . . death is coming now. It's . . . I'm so surprised by everything. I've lost the pain.

Carl then described the treatment of his dead body, which was pulled from the post where it had been pinned, disemboweled, and burned on a pyre of kindling. Unlike most of my patients, who tend to move from one death into the next life as they relate their experiences to me, Carl was able to follow the course his lifeless body took after death. Evidently his consciousness refused to leave the area where his body was located until the body was destroyed. I cannot account for this phenomenon but it was true of every incarnation Carl found during the entire course of his therapy.

With this first encounter we had found a link between Carl's impotence problem and his acute stomach pain, but the scene in no way played into the standard ulcer-causing problems of business and social worry. Carl continued to talk about "losing everything," but a second session failed to turn up any link with financial ruin, or social disgrace. Carl found himself in the prenatal period of another lifetime in some primitive civilization. The scene was an interesting replay of the first wife-stealing incident that Carl had described. In this lifetime, Carl's mother was engaging in illicit sex while he was in the womb. His father came upon the scene, pulled his mother's lover off his mother, and stabbed him. He then took a sword and ran it through Carl's mother and, simultaneously, through the fetus as well. The fetus was killed instantly, but the mother lingered long enough to hear the father screaming, "You'll never do that to me again! You'll never do it again!"

We had established the base of Carl's sex problem; he had learned that he was to "never do that again." He moved into a new lifetime, describing a well-appointed mansion in England and a staff of servants who tended him. I sensed that his business worries began here.

Sneaking up the stairs . . . back stairs, with a woman in a, you know, one of those little costume ball masks they hold up on a stick . . . we're kind of stumbling and giggling. Now we're in my bedroom and she makes me watch her get undressed, earring by earring, it takes so long. . . . Women wore . . . so much clothing, layers and layers of crinkly stuff beneath her dress. Now we're in bed and I'm on top of her; I'm naked too . . . and she says something in my ear . . . "What does it feel like to screw another man's wife?" And, God, suddenly I'm doubled up on the bed, my stomach just . . . it just pulled me over on myself, like a knife going in. That's my first instinct—she's stabbed me—but it's not true, it's just me. The pain, the pain.

What had happened to Carl was a direct restimulation of the earlier incident. Possibly he had an incipient ulcer that chose to strike at this particular moment. I would be inclined to argue, however, that this adulterous relationship caused a replay of his tribal life experiences. When his partner in crime whispered, "How does it feel to screw another man's wife?" his unconscious mind answered the question with a stabbing pain in the solar plexus. In other words, we have here a past life that is controlled by more remote past lives.

The woman, not wanting to be caught with Carl, promptly dressed and departed, leaving Carl on the bed with a stabbing pain in his upper abdomen. Eventually a doctor arrived, summoned by one of the servants. The diagnosis: a perforated stomach and a mild heart attack. He never fully recovered, however, and during his recuperation period, at a time when his investments needed careful and shrewd handling, he remained bedridden and unable to maintain control of his affairs. By the time he was able to assess the financial damage, he was perilously close to ruin. His doctor had prescribed belladonna, which Carl began to take in larger and larger doses. He became obsessed with regaining his fortune and began to hide cash all over the house, fearful that it would be taken from him in taxes. As his mental state deteriorated, he sought out fortune-tellers and card readers for advice on investments. Finally he was induced to bring a large sum of cash to a woman's house for a séance.

In a room with cloth hanging everywhere—I'm aware of certain suspicions about the evening, it's got to be a phony. The woman wears a cloth over her head and imitates voices from the dead. . . . There's just a sick feeling in my stomach . . . she's got all my money, and this is . . . nonsense what she's putting us through, and I look around the room at all these people with their hopes pinned on this . . . crazy woman . . . and it comes over me, what I've become.

I get up to go, grab my hat and coat, right in the middle of some nonsense she's going through, and I'm outside in a carriage. I've disrupted things, but now I'm outside . . . giving my address to the hackie . . . it's . . . Queensgate Gardens, somewhere, Fourteen Queensgate Gardens. But he pulls around into a kind of cul-de-sac, and before I can lean forward to ask what's happening two men are in the hack, poking a stick in my gut, saying, "Your money, let's have it," something like that, and I have almost none left, I've given it all to that woman. The stick pushes me back against the corner of the coach, they're searching me, a few coins, that's about all there is. I feel the pain, the pain, it's always there, burning up in my gut. Now I'm in the street. I guess . . . they threw me out. They're gone, everyone's gone. I'll walk . . . the best I can . . . walk home.

Carl's session evolved to a scene in his study, by his fireplace, with a dog at his feet. Many rooms of his home had been closed off to avoid heating costs and his household staff had been reduced to one servant.

There's nothing left, I am thinking, looking into the fireplace. I've . . . somehow I went off the track at a crucial moment. Now there's nothing left from everything I'd built up, except the belladonna, and I'm swallowing it all, by the fire. The pain goes first. Then the senses, and I'm drifting, everything is coming to a halt, all of my senses, the pain is gone. I'm pulling out, pulling out of the body, I can see the room, but I'm leaving it all behind, all my things, all my hidden cash, maybe no one will ever find it. I'm going up alone, over the room, leaving it all behind.

By the end of this session we had focused on the rather intricate connections between Carl's sex life and his business life, and the stomach pain associated with both. As he worked through these incidents he began to sleep better and to be less bothered by the pain. His worry over business continued, however, and he was troubled by an emotion which he expressed as, "I feel like they're coming to get me."

This phrase triggered him back to one of the most detailed and complete stories ever told to me by one of my patients. This life seemed to confirm the thesis that Carl's past lives were being governed by even earlier past lives. He described a Mexican plain, where he had lived for many years as a foreign-born national. Through a life of nearly ceaseless industry he had built up enormous ranch holdings and had become very powerful. He described an elaborate, teasing courtship with a woman who seemed to love him obsessively. They were married, and suddenly she turned cold, refusing to have sex with him, closeting herself with her brother for long periods of time. Carl became instantly suspicious of this woman, but he took no action, except to look for sexual satisfaction elsewhere. He found himself with a prostitute in an expensive hotel somewhere in an urban area. As he engaged in the sex act he realized that his wife had somehow followed him or arranged to be present.

"My wife knows, doesn't she?" he asked the woman. The response was silence, a turning away of the head. At this moment Carl experienced a sharp pain in his upper abdomen identical to the one he had suffered in England in his aristocratic past life. He made no connection between the two as he described the experience in Mexico, but I pointed out that he was describing similar patterns. In both cases I would attribute the attack to a replay of his lives in tribal communities where he was run through with weapons for the crime of illicit sex.

His infidelity in Mexico proved just as disastrous as it had in his English lifetime; his wife and her brother rushed into the room following his painful attack and, finding Carl in an adulterous sex act, had him taken to prison. Eventually, by bribing government officials, they arranged for his transfer to a mental hospital. In the process, they managed to take over all of Carl's holdings, and he was left destitute. His years in the institution, actually little more than a group of hovels, each containing a "patient," melded together in an inconsequential blur. He was able to replay his death vividly, however.

I'm in a room, a dark little concrete cell, and the dawn comes. There's a man, he brings me food and water. He opens the door this morning, like any other morning. He sets the stuff down—he gives me a horrible look. I haven't seen myself in God knows how long, there's no mirror or anything, and I can't. . . . I don't even know what I look like . . . but he screams, "Oh, my God . . . the plague!" and he slams the door. I don't know what's happened, I feel all right, but I sit thinking . . . they've done this to me, they'll come to get me yet, to finish me off. I know this isn't over . . . they're coming to get me. . . . I'm blinded by the light! It's midday and the door swings open. They're stuffing hay into my cubicle—unbaled, loose hay . . . I don't know what's going on, but more and more keeps coming in, and I know . . . they're doing this to me. My wife and her brother. Someone says, "We have to, you know . . . it's plague." And they touch a match to it and close the door.

Carl burned to death in the locked cell full of tinder-dry hay, fixed on one idea: He had lost everything and his life had been made torturous. He was convinced that his death was just one more sham, like the setup with the prostitute and the incarceration in the mental institution. He believed his life was controlled by enemy forces.

As we worked, finding other incidents like those described above, Carl realized that he did not *want* to own a business. He had gotten himself into the precarious life of owning and operating his own firm because he needed to play out his patterns of worry and loss. As we completed therapy, he was able to sell the electronics company and take a job with a large corporation. His life-style relaxed, his health improved and, as of this writing, his potential ulcer has never developed.

Carl Parson's case points up an interesting aspect of the therapist's job. Frequently it is the most off-center symptom of a patient's problem that will be the clue to helping him. It is in assessing the patient's problem, and not in curing it, that the therapist can be most helpful. Carl Parson *had* to do the work himself, as do all therapy patients. My function was simply to focus him on the fact that his impotence and his business failure were tied together. With that understanding he was able to find the links and successfully detach himself from the incidents that had controlled his life.

5

EPILEPSY

LEE ALLEN

DESPITE THE FACT THAT EPILEPSY HAS BEEN WITH US FOR thousands of years, and that the sufferer does nothing shameful to contract it, epileptics have always been social outcasts. They frighten people. The ever-present threat of a public seizure keeps even their friends at a distance. They frighten themselves as well, because their irregular attacks of convulsions seem to have no immediate cause or predictability. Although the condition is controlled by drug use, there is no cure.

I have treated many epileptics in an attempt to control their convulsions without a lifelong dependence on debilitating drugs. Results have been consistently good. Although no one can boast of a "cure" for epilepsy, I believe Past Lives Therapy has been as successful in reducing the number of seizures in epileptics as the phenobarbital and Dilantin that are normally prescribed. In at least one case, where drug treatment seemed to be backfiring, Past Lives Therapy discovered the reason.

Lee Allen was sixteen years old when she first came to me for treatment. She was at the age where a social life is just becoming important and the threat of failure is potent.

Lee had been through the embarrassing, unpredictable growth spurt that bewilders many adolescents but she was emerging on the other side as a graceful young woman. Despite this, she showed no signs of shedding her withdrawn personality and careless personal habits. She accepted life as an outcast; she was an epileptic. She had suffered convulsions since the age of two. Though heavy doses of phenobarbital and Dilantin were given to her, the seizures were not sufficiently under control to allow her a normal life. To compensate for her fear of being rejected she had begun having sexual relations with a variety of young men. She didn't enjoy such encounters and would have preferred not to engage in them. But because they offered her a kind of acceptance she was desperate for, she found herself unable to resist. Her homelife was a wreck. An alcoholic father dominated both her and her weak-willed mother. She fought regularly with her father, but to no avail; often the fights were followed by seizures.

In talking about her problems, Lee linked the seizures to her father, specifically to fights with her father. That was what we went after in our first session. Many patients recall long and detailed past-life scenes when the unconscious mind begins to play itself back, but Lee had a less complete picture of her previous lives. Crises flashed through her mind, piling up on each other, and it was not always easy to sort out the sequences she was talking about. This means of recall allowed me to see a rather complex pattern emerging, in which there was an extra element: The drug use that had become part of her daily life was itself causing the replay of several traumatic past-life incidents.

I asked Lee what she said to her father when he provoked her, and she recalled shouting at him, on more than one occasion, "You act like I'm here to die!" With this phrase prodding her unconscious, the following scenes grew out of each other.

"We're in a cemetery, this boy and me. I'm . . . sixteen. And we've . . . he's taken me to visit a grave, it's my mother's grave."

"Your mother is dead, then."

"Three days. She . . . took her own . . . she killed herself. She took pills."

"And this boy took you there?"

"I don't think so. I think I made him come there. He's trying to take me away now. 'Come on,' he's saying. 'That's enough.' But I'm kneeling on the grave and crying at him: 'Go away, I don't want you here, just leave me alone.' I'm here to die. When he goes, I have some pills. I planned this. They're the same pills . . . my mother had. I'm talking to her . . . telling her, 'I did it, I made you do this, I'll die like my mother died,' and I take the pills, swallow them, and lie down on the grave crying now, and I never . . . I'm never going to get up anymore . . . and—*What are you doing here?*!"

As Lee shouted this phrase I knew she had moved on, but the suddenness of the move took me by surprise. I had expected to play out this suicide with her, but there was no time.

"Who's saying that?" I asked. "Is that you?"

"A man, a man's caught me in a . . . some kind of bathroom, it's not really . . . there's no running water, just some pots, and towels and things. He's got me by the arm and he's shaking me. '*What are you doing here?*' "

"What *are* you doing there?"

"I don't know, I'm just telling him . . . I'm just here, that's all, I'm not doing anything. He's telling me: 'I thought I told you never to come back here, we don't want you here.' He's tearing me away, we're . . . at the top of some stairs, and he's hurting me, he's . . . hitting me. I'm down on the floor."

"Is he saying anything?"

" 'You can't do that with him, I told you I'd kill you both.' He's got my arms now and he's dragging me down the stairs. I hurt, and he's bumping my head, every step is hitting my head . . . Oh! . . . Oh! . . . Oh! . . ."

Here Lee let out a series of rhythmic shouts, and I knew she was experiencing the sequential blows to the head as she was dragged down a flight of stairs. We worked this violent assault several times before going on.

"I'm cramping now, I feel shooting pains all over and the convulsions are coming."

Lee described the humiliation of suffering an uncontrollable seizure while her tormentor watched.

"He drags me outside, down two more steps . . . leaving me there while I finish [the seizure]. He's shouting at me, 'No daughter of mine can do that with a man, you're no daughter of mine. I warned you!' "

As I had suspected, the man who beat Lee in this past life, caused her head injury, her seizures, and eventually her death, was her father.

Both of the abruptly terminated lives Lee worked through centered around conflicts between her parents and her lovers. In her present life, Lee's promiscuity found its source in her need to relive these unresolved conflicts. Her acute sense of humiliation over being epileptic seemed to grow out of the scene where her past-life father calmly watched her uncontrollable convulsions and ensuing death on the front steps of his house. Her use of drugs to induce death in the first life was somehow related to her current problems, but I was not sure how until she leapt unexpectedly from the scene on the steps into a third life. Suddenly Lee was describing a kitchen, in a more modern setting. She was a young drug addict and had just been let out of a prison-hospital.

That place is a joke. They took me there to withdraw. . . . I could choke on all the pills the orderlies were selling to the patients. Naturally I was no trouble to anyone. I didn't have to be. Now I'm home; there's a bottle in my purse. I've come down into the kitchen to get it. I can hear Mom and Dad . . . fighting in the bedroom. He's really letting her have it. About me. I'm trying to shut it out . . . that's all I want to do. . . . I'm taking the bottle, stuffing a bunch of tablets in my mouth, I just want them to shut up. Or to not hear them, or something. But I can't help listening. I'm circling the kitchen. He's saying, "You did this, you bitch, you forced her! She couldn't be what you wanted her to be, and you put the pressure on her." My mother, my mother admits it, she's just crying, saying, "I know, I know, she'll always be what she is now, it's awful, it's just awful." I'm wandering in a circle . . . it's taking effect. I'm losing touch with their argument, but I've taken too much, and I'm . . . drifting and—*now!*

"What's happened?"

"I've fallen, I'm whirling around . . . I've hit my head on . . . a counter, a . . . something, now I'm lying on my back and there's this blinding white . . ."

"What's white?"

"I guess, the ceiling is painted white. Maybe the light in the ceiling, I'm beginning to . . . it's happening again . . . the seizure . . . I can feel it coming, I can hear them talking . . ."

"What're they saying?"

"He's saying, she's lost now . . . she'll never be anything but what she is like now."

At this point in the session Lee experienced an epileptic seizure. I told her to move through it as if it were any other incident. The last words she played back before the seizure were those of her (past-life) father: "She'll never be anything but what she is now." Lee's unconscious mind had recorded the words and the action simultaneously. The meaning was clear: She would always be having seizures.

In these scenes we encountered all of the major themes contributing to Lee's convulsion pattern—beginning with a domineering, unreasoning, and violent father. Lee's relationship with her father in her present life was heavily influenced by the fact that her past-life father had physically assaulted her, causing her convulsions. Her current sexual behavior was the source of many fights with her father that were nearly identical to the one that led to her past-life assault. The scenes involving drug-taking, at her mother's grave and in the kitchen, made it clear to me why drugs were doing such a poor job in controlling Lee's seizures. Her past-life experience had "taught" her unconscious that drug-taking *caused* seizures rather than prevented them.

As the session continued, Lee quickly threaded her way to her prenatal period, in the eighth month of pregnancy.

Immediately we found a kitchen setting and a fight between her parents. Lee recalled that her father had forced her mother to swallow pills prescribed by the family doctor. Her mother turned away angrily, bumping her abdomen hard against a counter. The pain was sudden, almost causing her mother to pass out.

She's losing me! I feel like I'm falling, about to fall. I feel a . . . drain, like a feeling of support draining away from me. It's that same feeling when I'm about to have a seizure . . . everything pulling away. It's like a panic, I just want to cry, "Don't go! Don't lose me!" Then they're moving, to a bedroom, and I'm hearing them. He's saying, "I don't know how you expect me to pay for the hospital, you know there isn't any money."

This prenatal setting contained all of the patterns we'd been working with, the kitchen setting, the seizures, the drug use, and the father as "enemy" fighting Lee's existence. Although the scene seems minor, it was a cameo etched in detail, a concise moment when the past became tied to the present.

Throughout Lee's therapy we encountered difficulty in reaching the birth scene. The delivery room invariably drew a blank for Lee. Whenever I encounter this problem I know that something severe is lurking there. At the end of each session I would try to bring Lee into the moment of birth, but it was not until we had worked practically her entire prenatal period that she was able to re-experience that crucial phase of the life cycle.

"What are you feeling?" I asked.

"I want to get free. That's all. I want to get out, and I can hear a nurse or someone, a woman, saying 'push harder dear, it won't be long.' "

The delivery was a protracted affair. Lee's mother was unable to keep control of herself and was given several injections. The drugs had a positive effect on the mother; she relaxed enough to complete the delivery. For the emerging infant, however, the drugs were harmful in two interdependent ways.

> I feel like she's leaving me . . . I'm all alone. She's gone away. How can I do this alone . . . ? I'm frightened. Terrified—it's that feeling like the fits again . . . like everything's receding. Like right before I get a fit. It happened when they gave her that shot.

The "pre-convulsion" feeling induced by the drugs probably triggered several of Lee's more violent past lives. That the feelings were drug-induced was doubly unfortunate: It eradicated then and forever the possibility that drugs would help control Lee's seizures.

"I'm coming out, it's so bright, the room's white and my eyes hurt, the light is gleaming. White. Like clouds. Brighter than that ceiling, but the same. The same brightness."

"Are you hearing any words?"

"That woman . . . that nurse, she's saying, 'I bet your husband will be thrilled about the baby.' "

"And what's next?"

"My mother says, 'All I know is that when I get home I'm gonna grab him and have a fit!' "

I asked Lee to repeat this phrase. As she did, the mimicry of her mother's cadence was replaced by her own realization of the meaning of this scene and eventually by the perspective that is necessary to break the attachment.

Lee's therapy concluded with several reworkings of the birth scene. By the time she had finished working with me she was no longer taking any drugs to control her seizures and seemingly needed none. That was in the summer of 1972. In the spring of 1976 she checked in with me for a follow-up visit. She was the proud possessor of a driver's license, a piece of paper an epileptic does not win easily. She had not suffered a single seizure since the date of our last session (nearly four years) and had not used any anticonvulsant drugs during that time. For her the driver's license was a certificate of health; she no longer saw herself as society's outcast.

6

MALE SEXUAL PROBLEMS

HENRY AIKEN

IN SPITE OF THE SEXUAL REVOLUTION, OR PERHAPS BECAUSE of the revolution of rising sexual expectations, most people find it difficult to acknowledge a sexual problem. The media presentation of the sexually liberated man or woman is hard to live up to, and many find it almost impossible to admit that they fall short of that image. Traditional psychotherapy has had little success with sexual performance problems—premature ejaculation, failure to achieve orgasm, and impotence. Sex therapy, such as that described by Masters and Johnson, has fared better. Past Lives Therapy has uncovered a remarkable consistency in the patterns of patients suffering sexual dysfunction, and the rate of amelioration has been extraordinarily high.

"My wife won't have sex with me anymore," Henry Aiken explained to me at the beginning of his first session. "I guess that's why I'm here."

Henry looked as if he had once been a college football hero. At thirty-eight he was still tall, muscular, handsome, extremely well-groomed, and concerned with his appearance. The grooming was a kind of mask; Henry was trying desperately to keep his sexual problems hidden.

"This is my third marriage," he said. "I came too fast with my first wives, too. I think that's why they divorced me. They said it was for . . . other reasons."

Premature ejaculation is one of the most difficult sexual performance problems to treat by traditional therapy techniques. Frequently it persists long after all other problems, thought to be its cause, have been resolved. Many an otherwise salvageable marriage will crumble under the resulting pain and frustration; Henry's marriage was moving toward crisis.

I asked Henry to tell me what he felt like when experiencing his premature ejaculation.

"I feel like . . ." —he hesitated, because he knew what he said didn't seem to make sense—"I feel like I've got to hurry before someone catches me." He flushed. "It's kind of adolescent, isn't it? It's like someone keeps telling me, 'Hurry, hurry!' I always feel glad that I've come quickly, like I have had some kind of triumph, even though I know my wife is frustrated and unhappy. That triumph . . . it's just an emotion—it doesn't have anything to do with thinking about it."

Our session began with the phrase "Hurry, hurry!", the feeling of fear that he would be "caught," and the notion of triumph associated with the quick ejaculation.

"I hear a man's voice."

"All right. What is the man saying?"

"Hurry! Hurry!"

"Where are you? What are you doing?"

"I'm . . . uh . . ."

"Even if it's intimate or embarrassing, tell me what you're doing."

"I'm . . . doing it with this woman . . . a black woman. I'm . . . I'm black, too."

"Where are you?"

I'm not at home . . . I'm a slave. Home was a village, a warm, wet area . . . this must be Africa somewhere, but I don't know when. Our chief made a deal, some kind of deal with white traders, and I've been moved down the river, chained by the ankles to my tribesmen, and to others. We arrived at some kind of . . . I don't know what you'd call it now, a stockade I suppose, and they shoved us all together for days, my God the stink we throw up here! There's no . . . nothing like a bathroom or anyplace to go, we're just pigs in a pen. The temperature must have been in the nineties all night, the humidity combined with the stink. . . . Now they're shouting. . . . White men with clubs prodding us along down to the dock, shouting . . . the whole way: "Move along, hurry, don't take all day!" They poke at us on the outside of the group.

Now I'm standing before an open fire. There are several men in front of me in a line. They move up one at a time to be examined by the whites. It's my turn. I'm bewildered about what to do, but I'm walking forward. The white men examine my testicles, weighing them. They want to see if I'd make a good breed animal.

"This one will do," I hear a voice saying, and suddenly my neck collar is removed. I am branded on my right shoulder, placed in a cage on a wagon with the other "breeders," and brought to a boat.

Henry remembered nothing further about his boat trip. His mind immediately skipped to the unloading at a debarkation dock.

A line of white girls in broad hats standing on the dock watching us. We come off the boat and are stripped by white men. I feel like an animal, it's awful. Again we are prodded, but this time to a large open room, a dormitory.

As he described the room in which he was kept, Henry's face contorted.

"What are you feeling?" I asked him.

"Pain."

"What's causing it?"

"Whip. I'm being whipped. They bring women in. Sometimes I have to service three or four in the morning alone. More in the afternoon. The overseer times me with a whip."

"He's whipping you *while* you have intercourse?"

"He's shouting, 'This isn't for fun, you bastard, hurry up! If you can't come quick get off and let some other cock do it!' "

As Henry repeated this he continued to show the signs of the pain of the whip. For him the strap, the overseer's voice, and the issue of speed had become an integral part of sexual intercourse. A quick ejaculation would keep the overseer from beating him, his only triumph. His current sex life was a perpetual replay of this and other traumatic incidents.

I asked Henry to move forward to his death.

"I'm in my cell," he said, his face beginning to turn melancholy. "Two men come in. One of them owns me. They want me to masturbate."

"We want to make sure you're shooting something," my owner tells me. But I've climaxed six times today. I work at it, my God, it seems like hours are going by. The two men just stand in the door, glaring, it's almost impossible— and the only thought in my mind is, "If I don't come quickly, God knows what they'll do to me." But I can't. I just can't. I look up at them, terrified, still trying, but I know it's no use. It's impossible. My owner grunts and takes a kick at me. "You're too slow on a bitch, and you're too slow now. You've got to come quick if you want to stay alive."

I asked Henry to repeat the phrase.

"You've got to come quick if you want to stay alive," he said, carefully, two more times. The intensity drained from his voice and his facial muscles relaxed.

Now my owner's back. This must be some time later. He tells me that I haven't made any babies, and I'm worthless. They've sent me to a granary, strapped me to a large wheel. I don't think I ever had sex . . . again. In the middle of the night I wake up, people are crying outside: "Come quick! Get out or you'll die! Hurry! Hurry!" I open my eyes and I'm surrounded by flames. There's no way out. The heat is indescribable. The hot wind. The cinders. This is the end. And it's a relief. I'm running at the walls, and soon the flames are, I don't know, they've got me. The flames have got me. All around are voices shouting: "Come quickly! Hurry! Get out!"

To the unconscious mind, of course, the phrases used at

the time of Henry's death had the same meaning as those used during his sexual torture; the two meanings of the word "come" were not differentiated. At death he unconsciously sensed that he was being punished because he did not "come quickly."

This past life, the first one that Henry Aiken reached, seemed to be the root of his problem, but it was, of course, not an isolated experience. The death by fire led him directly into another lifetime.

Two boys in a barn. One of them is a friend, and the other is me. We're, you know, showing our genitals to each other. . . . We're talking about how you "do it" with girls, I guess we must be thirteen. We're . . . masturbating. And this friend, I think his name is Mark . . . ? Marcus, maybe, he's saying, "If you stroke it slower it'll take longer." But I think that's kind of silly, I guess girls would like it if we got it over with quickly, and they didn't have to be bothered. He thinks that's funny, but I think girls can't possibly like sex. Now my mother calls: "If you boys are smoking up in that loft, I'll strap you both. You boys'll burn that barn down, I swear." Suddenly I panic; I leap up. "Come on," I say, "put it away quick! They might catch us and then they'll beat my ass."

This small, seemingly insignificant scene is remarkable in that its details encompass nearly every element of Henry's past life as a slave. The discussion of sexual attitudes, Henry's certainty about the superiority of a quick ejaculation, and the suggestion of fire and "burning" all led him to exclaim, "Come on, quick . . . or they'll beat [me]." All of these events, none of them important in itself, played out in a coincidental time sequence that brought Henry in contact with his earlier life of horror. As a result, this minor incident had been permanently stamped on his unconscious mind. It was followed by a similar scene, also a miniature:

I'm in a small attic somewhere. It's hot, stuffy. I'm in my teens, and there's a girl there with me. She's naked, and she's saying, "Hurry up and do it before someone catches us!" I tell her it's impossible, it's not hard yet, and she begins to . . . masturbate me. "I'll get it hard for you," she says, but I tell her, "It's no use, you'll never get me hard that way." Next she says, "Well, do something. We've got to hurry." Just then we hear voices; I hold my hand over her mouth. "Hurry," she whispers. "We've got to get out of here quick."

In the prenatal period of this lifetime, Henry found his parents engaging in sex. It was not a happy experience. His mother's thoughts were these: "I hope he comes quick and leaves me alone. I hate it when he goes on for a long time. I never climax anyway, I'd rather do him by hand, but that takes even longer."

This incident led into a delivery room scene where we found the doctor saying to a nurse, "Maybe we'll be lucky. Maybe he'll come quickly. She'll feel better if it comes quick and gets out of there."

Once again an innocent enough statement has played back the phrases that controlled Henry's past lives. The disorder of premature ejaculation is locked in.

Henry worked a total of eight sessions. After the fifth he had his first sexual breakthrough. He had sustained intercourse long enough to give his wife a satisfying climax, and her pleasure was so flattering that their sex life began to regenerate at a remarkable rate. Three final sessions cleared out the remaining reinforcements, and gave us time to monitor his improvement.

7

FEMALE SEXUAL PROBLEMS

SARAH FOSTER

FAILURE TO ACHIEVE ORGASM IS A PROBLEM ALMOST EVERY woman suffers at some time in her life. For many, it is a passing disorder, associated with an unhappy relationship or a particularly depressing period of life. But for others it is a constant fact of life, a debilitating, demeaning block to happiness and fulfillment. For Sarah Foster it was also associated with physical pain and increasing depression.

Sarah was twenty-three years old, with long dark hair and a thin, vulnerable face. She wore no makeup and dressed in a uniform of blue jeans, sandals, and an Indian blouse. She presented herself as free-spirited, independent, and unconcerned with what the world thought about her. Our first interview revealed her tenuous hold on this posture:

> I'm terrified that someone will get too close to me. I want to fall in love, I feel like . . . there's all this love inside, but . . . I freeze when a man walks up to me. I swallow and words get caught in my throat. . . . All I keep thinking is "Don't touch me . . . don't put a hand on me. . . ." I know that's crazy. I mean, when I get to know a man and we make love, it's so confusing . . . I have a pain. I feel like I'm approaching some sort of climax, and then there's this stabbing pain, and then I cry. Now I'm afraid to do it anymore. I mean, you just can't do that to men over and over . . . they have rights, too.

Sarah was experiencing one symptom unrelated to all this sexual trauma—she awakened regularly at about four in the morning with acute abdominal cramps. She could see no connection between the cramps and her failure to achieve orgasm, but I felt there had to be some tie-in. I made a note of it but decided not to pursue it, hoping that Sarah would come to it herself during the session.

I asked Sarah what it was she most feared in getting close to a man. She thought for a moment, and gestured with her hands when she could find no words. Finally she blurted out, "I'm afraid I'll never be able to break out. I'm afraid it will put me in a rigid situation, and I'll just be stuck there. That doesn't make sense, does it?"

"Everything you say makes sense," I said. "I'm just not sure what it means. If you found yourself stuck someplace—physically stuck, unable to break out . . . if your body were rigid, what could you tell me about it? The first thing coming to mind—where are you?"

I can't stand up and I can't sit down. I'm . . . isn't anyone going to get me out of this? Isn't anyone going to help me?

It's a cage, like an animal cage at the zoo, but it just fits down over me. I can't move—I'm squatting. It's too low to stand up, too narrow to fit. It isn't fair. He never wanted me. He just wanted to use me . . . to own me.

Sarah had found herself in an early civilization. As she backtracked to pick up the circumstances surrounding her imprisonment, we found she was being punished by a husband for having sex with another man. Human life was not highly valued, and he did not particularly care if the punishment killed her. She had been in this cage for days.

As this life began to evolve, I was faced with several odd occurrences. The first was that Sarah began to speak a language that neither of us had ever heard before. It sounded to the untrained ear like an African tribal tongue, but Sarah's speech was so erratic that we could not concentrate on the sounds of the language enough to define it. As fascinating as this situation was, I was frankly more interested in solving Sarah's sexual problem than in pursuing an oddity. I simply told Sarah to translate the meanings for me as she heard the people around her talking. From time to time she would slip back into the tongue, but a gentle suggestion resulted in a translation.

I don't know how long I've been here, I don't even know where I am really. Three men are taking me out of my cage now . . . taking me to a wide spot in the woods. This is all outdoors . . . hot . . . almost steamy. A man waits for me . . . my husband. He's telling me I disgraced him . . . I'm just a whore, a slut . . . but I don't see what he's talking about. . . . He never showed any interest in me, never paid any attention to me. Now . . . My God, he's got a whip, and . . . Oh God!

Sarah thrashed twice on the couch, and again we encountered something that I find difficult to explain. As she continued to tell me her experiences, red welts began to appear across her cheek, chin, and shoulders. These marks lay in parallel lines across her, as they would if she had been whipped with a cat-o'-nine-tails. I was mystified by this physical manifestation of past-life injury. Again I felt that our focus should be Sarah's troubling emotions, rather than the pursuit of inexplicable phenomena. We proceeded, simply taking note of the physical symptoms, which receded as the session continued.

I beg him for mercy. But he doesn't even hear me. He tells the men, "Put her back in the cage." I'm crying to him . . . "No, no, I'll die in there!" But he looks so bland. He doesn't even respond.

They've put me back. I'm squatting again, and it's killing me. The pain is excruciating.

I asked for a description of the pain. The response was as I expected.

It's the pain in the stomach . . . lower, actually. The pain in the abdomen. I feel it every night. It's my four A.M. pain. That's it. It's from squatting.

Now I'm being led to a room. I told him I would do anything . . . anything to get out of the cage, and finally he's relented. They're bathing me and it feels so good. Hot water swirling up around my middle. I just want to stay forever . . . but I can't. They're giving me a drink. . . . "It's for the pain," someone says. For the pain . . . what pain?

In another room. I'm lying back on a pallet, a low straw bed, and there are tools. I can see them so clearly . . . knives, scissors . . . they're so beautiful: gold shafts, carved with blue . . . some kind of blue inlays. They're like jewelry, almost. I wonder . . . why do I remember them so clearly? Nothing else is that clear . . . but I'm getting drowsy. . . . My husband is there. . . . He's saying to another man . . . a doctor . . . "I hope this helps me." And the doctor says, "It never fails. We just have to cut quickly to avoid the pain. She'll never care about finishing again."

Sarah described a sharp stabbing pain in her vaginal area, a pain that caused her to pass out. When she returned to consciousness she heard the doctor advising her husband, "Don't use her for a few days. We don't want infection to set in."

Suddenly Sarah became very excited. She began to speak more rapidly, describing her current life. She was suffering from a vaginal yeast infection that she had neglected to mention to me in her initial interview. She had suffered with this disorder for five years; it had become a part of her daily life. It had not responded to medication, which normally clears up such infections in a matter of weeks. We reworked and repeated the doctor's statements until Sarah felt she could move on.

I'm recovered now, and I don't care about sex at all. He uses me when he wants to, but I don't feel a thing. I cry all the time, I feel like I'm half human. I can't react to anything. Nothing matters. Then I remember . . . those knives. The tools in the operating room. They're so pretty,

so . . . desirable. It's night. I'm sneaking into the room.
I don't think I've seen it since the . . . operation. I don't
know how long it's been. I don't know anything about
what happened in between. But there they are. A golden
knife. Blue flowers. I'm taking it in my hand . . . it goes
in right at the center of the abdomen. My God . . . it
hurts so much. I wish I hadn't . . . it hurts.

I'm on the floor now, and I know I'm dying. I'm dying.
I'm thinking . . . "All I wanted was to be loved . . . it
shouldn't have led to all this. All I wanted was to be
loved."

In reworking these experiences, Sarah found the similarities between past and present. She had recently broken off a
relationship with one man and started seeing another. Her
first boyfriend was furious about the new relationship, and
berated Sarah over the phone constantly. His behavior
frightened her and made her feel guilty. Although the old
boyfriend was powerless to physically punish Sarah, mental
tormenting played neatly into this past life and suicide.

From this early civilization Sarah moved to somewhere in
the United States, during the early western expansion. In a
primitive western town, populated by hardworking, hard-
drinking men, she was a bar waitress and sometime prostitute.

I feel a pulling, like the people pulling me out of the
baths before, but it's a man . . . at the bar. He's pulling
me toward this long flight of stairs, and I'm going. But
I don't understand. I'm confused about what's going on
here. I seem to be a prostitute but I don't feel like I know
what I'm doing. I must be very young. I guess that's it.
I'm just sort of dazed, going up the stairs. This man is
very gentle. He seems kind of . . . nice. He's taking me
to a bedroom. He's very gentle. We're undressed, and I'm
slowly very . . . excited, aroused. We're making love, I
can feel a climax approaching. It's a very close thing, I
can't see how I can be a prostitute. I really like this man
. . . I feel very tender, and excited at the same time. . . .

It's . . . it's . . . Oh lord, he's finished. He's finished. He's pulling away from me . . . I'm so confused, I was, like, in a dream with him. Now he's off the bed already. Getting into his clothes. I'm still lying there, feeling like . . . "What happened?" He looks down at me and he says, "Jesus, you're some whore! You're not good enough for *any* man." He throws a coin on the bed, and leaves. I'm all alone. Crying, angry. Still confused. Why doesn't anyone love me?

Sarah described dressing and going back out into the hall above the bar. She was so disoriented from the experience that she had neglected to tie her shoes, and she tripped at the top of the stairs. Falling the entire flight, she struck her head against the banister post at the bottom. Her last vision was from the floor; the man she had just made love to was sitting at the bar, and turned around momentarily to see what all the commotion was about before turning away with a shrug. She was taken back upstairs and left without medical attention. By morning she was dead.

This incident crystallized the mistrust Sarah felt for all men. The moment before climax had become a focal point of trauma for her in her current life. It was the moment when she knew she would be betrayed and left alone.

As we moved into the prenatal period of Sarah's present life, we found a related incident in the seventh month. Her parents were engaged in sex, but her mother found the experience repulsive and painful.

She's thinking, "Don't touch me there. You act like an animal. Leave me alone. . . . I don't get anything out of this—God knows how long it's been since I came." Now she's rolling over. He's groaning and coughing, lying on his back . . . and she's thinking, "If I can help it he'll never touch me again."

Despite the strength of this scene, Sarah did not seem ready to leave the prenatal period. We worked many similar scenes of animosity between her parents, but at no point did she really become detached from the situation in the womb. Finally, when we had spent several sessions reworking incidents that we had seen before, we struck a new event. Sarah's mother was in the hospital, awaiting delivery. She had checked in early, and was looking for something to read.

My father's coming into the room. He's eating something, I guess . . . a hamburger or something, because mother's looking at him, and her stomach's turning over. He's saying, "You found something to read." She says, "Yes, it's very strange. It's called *Philosophy in the Bedroom*, by the Marquis de Sade." He's never heard of it. He asks her, "What's so strange about it?" and she reads him a few sentences.

Sarah put her hands over her eyes and slowly recited the following passage, which is indeed from *Philosophy in the Bedroom*:

What well made man, what man endowed with vigorous organs, does not desire, in one way or another, to molest his partner during his enjoyment of her? I know perfectly well that whole armies of idiots, who are never conscious of their sensations, will have much trouble understanding the systems that I want to establish. What do I care for these fools?

Hold her, and expose her arse, as I will plunge into it. And I will kiss her with a cat-of-nine-tails, which she must surely learn to love and find stimulating. Would you do me the great kindness, madam, of allowing me the great pleasure of biting and pinching your lovely flesh while I am fucking with thee?

Her ability to recite this passage, presumably from unconscious memory, left both of us somewhat breathless. We went over the passage several times, detaching her slowly and carefully. Interestingly, the attitudes in it echoed her own feelings of what men believed about women in general, her in particular. At the end of this intense period of concentration Sarah was limp, but serene. She at last felt free of these crippling ideas.

Although Sarah had heard of the Marquis de Sade, for whom sadism was named, she claimed to have no familiarity with his work, nor any knowledge of when he lived, what his philosophy consisted of, or whether it was available in print. Her recollection of this passage which her mother read aloud immediately prior to giving birth was the third inexplicable occurrence in her therapy. Other phenomena of this type will be dealt with in more detail in the last part of this book, in the chapter "Inferences, By-products, Implications."

Sarah's first painless sexual encounter occurred within days of the "de Sade" session. The early morning abdominal cramps and the vaginal yeast infection had disappeared earlier in therapy. This sudden "break" with the symptoms of pain and guilt is in the typical resolution of a sexual problem.

Sexual difficulties, often inaccessible to traditional therapists, are among the most easily solved problems I encounter in Past Lives Therapy. Most require a very few sessions. Unfortunately, when a sexual impasse occurs in a relationship, it is sometimes masking a deeper problem in that relationship, and often it becomes a scapegoat for all of the difficulties two people have with each other. In cases where the sexual problems have been solved and the relationship does not improve sufficiently, we must go into the dynamics of the relationship itself.

8

RELATIONSHIPS

THE GORDONS

LOVE AT FIRST SIGHT: DOES IT EVER REALLY HAPPEN? TWO people spot each other in a crowd, and suddenly they *know* —they have found a mate for life. Frequently their judgment is incorrect, but this doesn't lessen the initial emotional impact. Where does that "pull" come from? At the risk of deflating many romantic dreams, I suggest that some people have been together in past lives. In this life they unconsciously recognize each other. This may seem unlikely, but my experience working with couples indicates that some have known their mates for an extraordinarily long time.

Carl and Abigail Gordon came to me because their relationship was taking wild turns neither one of them could understand. In their early forties, they appeared to be the average American couple—slightly overweight, slightly too involved in their careers, but by no means abnormal. This appearance masked a living hell.

ABIGAIL:

He belittles me in front of our friends, he points out our religious differences at parties, and shuts me out when our friends are around. He's always playing games with me, taunting me, threatening me with "another woman," who never materializes. I can't have children—I'm afraid of what he'd do to them with these psychological games he plays. But even so, I don't want sex with anyone else . . . I really love him.

CARL: I really love her, but she infuriates me. Little things drive me crazy. . . . I can't stop myself from needling her, making her see how she does things wrong. . . . I know I play games with her . . . God knows she tells me often enough . . . but I can't stop. I love her and I hate her. Sometimes I think . . . I'd rather, or, not rather, but *if* I had a relationship with a, um . . . a man, it might be better. But I don't want a man sexually necessarily. Some men are a little attractive to me, but . . . I guess I'm afraid of the whole thing. I don't want to feel kinky, but I do play these games with Abby. I know she hates it.

My work with Carl and Abigail was conducted in separate sessions. I feared that in a joint session they would try to change each other, rather than concentrate on each taking responsibility for his or her own patterns. I wanted to isolate Abigail from Carl, but I discovered that isolating them physically did not keep them entirely apart. The following edited transcripts are labeled with the name of the speaker.

ABIGAIL: . . . I see a thick, black wall. I'm looking over from the outside. I see fields outside. Open space. Inside the wall is a ruined garden. There's a pool, a wading pool, Now I hear a gong. I'm supposed to go inside, and I'm thinking, "He wants me to serve him. I'm not going, I'll just sit here." Oh my God! Screaming . . . someone's screaming from inside. I'm rushing in and the man. . . . It's Carl, I know it is, I can just tell. He's cutting another one of his wives. We're all his wives. There's a lot of us. He's got one down on the ground, and he's cutting her back with a knife. He turns around and faces me. "Come here . . ." he says, and he's speaking very softly, but there's a look in his eye . . . he's crazy, he's flushed from cutting this woman. She's dead, and the other wives drag the body out. Now he's pointing to me. "Come here, come here."

"I don't have to," I'm shouting, and this fury is in his eyes. The other wives have come back, and they're starting to scream, too. I grab a torch from a holder, and I thrust it at him. His clothes are on fire, and I'm running after him. The flames are leaping all around him. He throws himself into the pool, and I'm in after him . . . holding his head down. He's stopped moving now . . . he's dead.

CARL: . . . . It's a small town . . . all adobe buildings . . . this must be . . . Syria? Somewhere like Syria but we're a tribe. It's not our town, we're riding through . . . twelve of us. I'm the leader, and I ride first. I see a woman at a well. She's looking up as we ride in. She's curious, but she looks . . . nervous.

The men gather around the well. "We'll have a little fun," I tell them as we surround the girl. But I'm thinking, I can't let this go too far—she's probably got a whole town of soldiers set to defend her. But still . . . we've got to have a *little* amusement.

"Twelve could make it interesting for you," I say as we ride up. She turns around, frightened. She's looking for a way out. But my men are too quick for her . . . the horses close in wherever she turns. "We haven't had a woman for a long time," I say. "Twelve is better than one." Her eyes are darting around, and I'm laughing.

But oh, my God, they're on us! A horseback . . . army. They've spotted us while we were at the well. I spin around but it's too late. They're on top of us. Someone is taking me from my mount. Two men. They've grabbed me. There's a cliff at the edge of the well, and I'm being—Oh, God! Falling.

Carl's breath became short, as if someone had kicked him in the stomach. In fragmented sentences he related his death as he landed on a rock in a ravine.

The patterns that emerged in these two incidents expressed the essential "ground rules" of Carl and Abigail's life together. Although Carl did not identify the woman at the well as Abigail, he treated her in much the same manner that he treated his wife. I seldom find couples identifying their mates in past lives; I expected Abigail's identification to be an isolated instance. But the pattern of the relationship was to become more complex:

ABIGAIL:

A hotel room . . . long ago. There's no electricity, we have a gas jet burning on the wall. I'm naked and a young man is tickling my feet. We're both naked. I've run away from my father. This man has taken me away but I don't like him. Still, we're . . . doing it, but I don't feel anything. Then he falls asleep. I'm crying. I don't think I know what is happening to me. I'm very young. I'm going to go out. I really don't know what I'm doing.

On the street, I'm aware of a carriage looming above me. A man gets out. He takes my hand, apologizes. He's very genteel, and I feel a strong pull toward him, although there's something . . . mysterious about him. He's taking my dress in his hand . . . where the carriage splashed mud on it. And he's saying, "Why don't you come with me, let me get you cleaned up." I don't know what to do. But this man is so . . . he's almost magnetic. Now I'm getting into the carriage.

A feeling of anticipation. I'm now in an office making marks on a paper. I still don't know what I'm agreeing to, exactly, but I get room and board. I think I sense . . . this man isn't normal. But I'm taken to a pretty pink room, and given nice clothes . . . everything I could want.

Someone wakes me up. It's the middle of the night. A woman says I'm "wanted." Taken down a long hall, to an open door. This man's inside, dressed in black. I walk over to him and stumble over his outstretched legs. He laughs and catches me, and he slams the door. It's completely black. Now he lights a candle, and I can see —the walls are lined with torture instruments. And he says, "We're going to play a little game. It's called the 'scare you to death' game."

He walks me along the wall, past whips, knives, pistols, and his hand is digging into my shoulder. "Now you must play," he says, and I scream.

At this point Abigail described a series of teasing sex acts, in which the man paid no attention to her, except to use her and terrify her. Her fear and discomfort seemed to excite him more than any physical contact, but ultimately he was unsatisfied, and threw her out. At this point let us pick up Carl's session.

CARL: There's a stupid girl. I've called her in. This house I run, it's famous because I guarantee that I can satisfy any desire, any fantasy. And this is a boomtown full of wild men. . . . San Francisco seems to stick in the mind . . . I feel like I'm in San Francisco. My life here . . . I'm terrified that my mother will find out what I do. I . . . have to find excuses to keep her away, and my life is a nightmare. I . . . it's harder and harder to excite me. My girls . . . I call them slaves. They have to submit to what I say. But this girl is new, she's stupid, and she annoys me. I have her in a room, it's what pleases me—a black room where she can't see me and doesn't know what will happen next. And she's saying, "Please, I don't want to play the game," and I'm telling her, "You've got to play the game, this is our little fun game." There are whips and things on the wall, for me to use, but with this girl it's not worth it. She's obstinate and annoying.

Carl's description of his sex acts with the girl in his black room paralleled Abigail's description.

But it's no good. I just can't get any satisfaction. Finally I just throw her out. There's a woman outside who takes her and I tell her, "She'll never play the game, just take her to the farm." In her place I have a boy brought in.

The scene, which Carl and Abigail described in separate sessions, seems likely to be from the same life, although up until this point they did not state that they recognized each other. The scene focused Carl's fears of latent homosexuality, which he had attempted to gloss over in our original interview. All of his "game playing" in this past life seemed to be tied to tormenting women and then satisfying himself with boys. The scene brought Abigail in contact with her pattern of submissiveness. She hated Carl's behavior toward her, but she felt powerless to do anything about it, or even to try. After this session she began to take a much stronger attitude toward her husband, and the marriage began to move toward a balance of wills.

Abigail fully described the "farm" that Carl mentioned in his session. She had evidently been sent there to live. It was located several miles behind the brothel that Carl ran, and both Carl and Abigail died there on the same night. Abigail had been sent there to join the other "inadequate" prostitutes, and those who had had children. It was a working farm, which Carl operated as a profitable business.

As Carl ran through more and more perverse sexual games he became harder and harder to satisfy. Finally the night came when neither girl nor boy could excite him. In a rage, he took his horse and rode to the farm.

CARL: I've called them out. Every girl on the farm, and the one I want . . . the one I hate . . . that girl from the black room. I know her. It's Abby. It's Abigail, but it doesn't look like her. She's the one I want. All the women are watching. I'm still on the horse, and I ride at her, stopping short. She falls. I can see this is taking hold of me. She's terrified, and I can't stop. "You wouldn't play my games!" I shout. "All this is your fault!" I get down from the horse. There's a hook . . . like a meat hook, but it's used for hauling bales of hay. It's sharp, and it hangs on the wall. I'm pushing her back, back, sinking her onto it. Everyone's watching. . . . And now, at last I'm aroused, because it's going to kill her. That's what I keep thinking. It's going to kill her.

Carl described his sexual excitement during this torture/death as being totally tied to his simultaneous love-hate of the woman on the baling hook. She was giving him the greatest orgasm of his life, but, in dying, she was also taking the experience with her, never to be repeated.

This situation was infuriating. Carl felt devotion and hatred simultaneously. He could not stand the idea that this woman somehow controlled his pleasure and happiness. He replayed this abusive pattern with Abigail in their present life, stopping short of the physical violence he had inflicted in the past.

As the sessions progressed Carl lost the need to hurt his wife. The taunting, the game-playing, and all of the mechanisms he had used to destroy her self-respect were remnants of an inappropriate past situation. The present was not nearly as threatening. His homosexual impulses seemed to disappear as his marriage stabilized.

Abigail's patterns of submissiveness were equally inappropriate to her in this life. Her inability to leave Carl or to change him was a replay of a life where she had been *physically* restrained from doing either. When this situation became clear to both of them their relationship seemed to adjust naturally. Because they basically loved each other, and did not want to part, we worked to eliminate their destructive behavior toward each other. In some cases, where couples have come together without love, but purely because of a past-life attachment, I make no attempt to unite them. I believe it is healthier for them to free themselves of the attachment so that they can seek more appropriate mates.

The case of Carl and Abigail is quite unusual. I seldom ask for such recognition experiences, and I seldom receive them voluntarily from my patients. Where they do occur, they make for most interesting work.

Carl and Abigail ultimately formed a lasting business partnership and, by trusting Abigail with matters of financial responsibility, Carl put his newfound respect for her into action. It took Abigail some time to adjust to this level of responsibility, and the relationship was slow to settle into a healthy pattern. One of the hardest facts for a therapist to face is that, by bringing a patient into direct confrontation with his life *as it really is,* he may make it harder, rather than easier, for that patient to live. Usually this is a temporary situation, but it can be painful to watch. I must continue to believe, however, that a healthy human being is better than a sick one, and that a person facing a tough reality is more alive than one who has adjusted to cowering in a world controlled by the past.

9

~ALCOHOLISM

BEN PLUMMER

THE EXACT PHYSIOLOGICAL NATURE OF ADDICTION IS UNKNOWN.
Treatment of addicts has advanced, though it is by no means
scientific. I have worked with many drug addicts and alco-
holics, and the kinds of past-life incidents they recall are quite
similar. Whatever the addict is addicted to, his past will be
replete with instances where an outside substance, introduced
into the body, solved some problem. The "problem" will
often be the pain of death.

Although this chapter deals specifically with alcoholism,
it provides a general example of the kinds of past-life patterns I find in my work with addicts.

Ben Plummer had lost all motivation by the time he came
to me for treatment. He had been a business manager of a
large but failing wholesale house owned by a very powerful
woman. He had turned the business around, bringing it to
its first profitable quarter in years, only to be pushed out
by the owner, who began to suspect that he would use his
success to control her. It was at the moment he realized he
was being edged out of position by a woman that Ben
Plummer began to drink. His descent was dramatic and
seemed irreversible. In a matter of months he was mixing
his morning coffee with vodka to hide the delirium tremens
that awakened him each day. In a year he had been hospital-
ized in an expensive sanitarium that catered to the upper-
class alcoholic with a reputation to protect. This treatment
proved disastrous, sending Ben into a nearly psychotic de-

pression. He had just completed his stay when we had our first interview.

"If I go back to the hospital," he said, "I'll never come out alive. I'll die right there."

Ben shook his head back and forth very slowly throughout our interview. I knew this indication of hopelessness was in part designed to cover the slight trembling movement of his head when he attempted to hold it still. It cast a bleak atmosphere over the scene nonetheless.

"I seem to be able to work my brain," Ben said sadly, "but I can't move. I just watched the rug pulled out from under my feet. Everything I had built was destroyed . . . sometimes I think I'm dead already. Just my body is here to keep up appearances."

We evolved Ben's first past-life incident from these phrases. He described a large empty concrete room, with a persistent dripping noise.

> I'm naked. I'm just a boy. I'm all alone. I think my mother put me here. Some kind of institution . . . a prison or something. I don't know what's happened to put me in this place. Something about . . . my brother is dead. I didn't kill him . . . but that's why I'm here. They think I killed him. Or we went someplace together and he's dead, and it's my fault. . . . I'll never get out. They've left me here forever . . . I just want to end it. Stop brooding on it. I'm . . . banging my head against the walls. Oh God, it hurts. But there's a rhythm to it. I want my brain to stop. Stop thinking about all this. I'm just trying to crack it open . . . that's all. Crack it open.

Death, from a brain concussion, occurred in the emergency room of this prison hospital. This incident gave me one avenue to pursue that I might have otherwise overlooked: A woman had put Ben in the concrete room. He chose to point this up. It was a woman whose business machinations had triggered his alcoholism. I suspected we would encounter more examples of female betrayal. Ben was not inclined to follow this path immediately, however. He recognized that

this incident partially explained his fear that he would die
in the hospital. He followed it with a similar, more amplified
life, in Japan or China.

This room is ornamental . . . high ceilings, faint scenes
painted on the walls . . . but I'm still alone. There's a
man coming in. I'm tied up. He hands me a bowl with
something in it. It looks like cereal. "Take this," he says.
"It will make it easier for you. You will be redeemed for
your evil acts. This will help." He leaves now. This stuff
smells. It's like rice, but it's red . . . there's . . . I think
it's fermented. I'm eating it, or drinking it. There's liquor
in it, but it tastes awful. Still . . . I'm getting hazy. I'm
beginning to get dizzy. I'll never get out of here alive.
Never. This part isn't too clear. They're coming to get
me. Taking me away. I'm in a different room. I'm tied
to a board. A man is feeding me more of that stuff . . .
saying, "This will bring honor out of what you've done."
They've cut me. They're cutting me open. It hurts. It's
killing me.

In all likelihood the statement "this will bring honor out
of what you've done" referred to the pain Ben was about
to undergo. But, because of the juxtaposition of events, his
unconscious mind recorded the phrase and the act of drinking simultaneously. It was the first of many incidents involving praise of alcohol. He described a fatal wound in a
mine explosion; his cohorts washed his wounds with corn
whiskey and fed him from the same bowl, repeating the
phrase, "There's nothing like a good bottle of booze, there's
just nothing like it." He recalled an incident from early
childhood, a fishing trip with his father. They joined a group
of men who got drunk around a picnic table. To quell his
fear of these men, Ben indulged in his first bottle of beer.
The men encouraged him, pounding him on the back, shouting, "There's no problem ain't made easier with a good
bottle of beer!"

This childhood incident, which ended in dizziness and

collapse, led directly to a past life in which Ben operated a carrousel.

> In Germany, I think, or Bavaria. I open up this little merry-go-round in a small park about two o'clock in the afternoon . . . run it till about sundown. The dizziness . . . I recognize that feeling, when I collapsed at the picnic table. It's from looking at the kids going around and around on this merry-go-round. That's all I do for those four or five hours a day. Pack up at about seven . . . I have a little room nearby. A basement place—no windows. Go on back, sit on my bed and drink beer. Drink and drink, waiting to sleep. Then I sleep a few hours and have a few more. Then sleep. Just like the carrousel . . . around and around. Drinking and sleeping. Till it's time to open up again. That's all I do. That's my whole life.

At the end of the session, reflecting on the carnival life, Ben told me the following:

> When I was in the hospital a psychiatrist told me something that I reacted to very violently. He said, "You've become addicted to your pain." I really exploded at him—I'm not sure why—but I felt that dizzy feeling. Like the feeling this life started with. I think it was that dizzy sense of life going around and around . . . addicted to my life-style of drinking and working.

This seemed to be an astute analysis of Ben's situation, but I felt his violent reaction to the doctor's phrase "addicted to your pain" probably had even more direct roots. Ben's carrousel-operator life-style was a kind of symbolic addiction. In Past Lives Therapy we try to remain on a literal level, and I felt we would come upon a scene of genuine addiction. At the beginning of Ben's next session, we found a life that encompassed the disparate elements of his problem.

> My wife caught me. I always knew she would. I'm in a place . . . it's like the hospital I just got out of . . . for

rich people with . . . problems. But I think it's because
of women, not drink. She's found out I'm having an affair.
I guess I'm drinking, too . . . but this place isn't for my
own good. She wants me out of her hair. They bring me
liquor when I want it in here. . . . I think this is the
early eighteen hundreds. They dress formally. Giving me
glasses of brandy mostly. I think I have a good deal of
money. I'm drinking the brandy, but it doesn't go down
easily—I'm thinking of her, how she did this to me.

We had discovered this resentment of women before. Now
the festering of the emotion seemed to be the "pain" that
Ben was addicted to.

They put something . . . there's a substance in the
brandy. . . . I know because they're sloppy about the
time, and when they're late my palms begin to sweat.
That's withdrawal . . . I feel I know it. I've been violent.
They're putting something in the drink to calm me. They
don't want to make me better, just keep me under wraps.
I get headaches when they're late with the booze. I start
to shake.
    I can't concentrate anymore. Time has gone by—I can
see my skin has gotten scaly. There's no more brandy.
They just bring a bucket . . . it looks like a farmer's milk
pail. Sweet wine and opium. There's a man bringing it.
I don't complain anymore . . . I'm used to it. He says,
"This is one way to get rid of your problems, if you don't
mind where you go or how you get there." I'm just nod-
ding at him . . . all I want is the bucket. I don't think
I can reach it, though. It's so sudden. All at once I'm dying.
Just giving out all over. I think I'm dead.

Here the three thrusts of Ben's emotional peril—the dominant woman ruining him, the fear of dying in the hospital,
and the addiction to his situation, played themselves out in a
quiet, ignoble death. The ever-present advice in favor of
alcohol, spoken on this occasion by a hospital orderly, as-

sured Ben's future addiction. From here Ben moved to the birth into this life.

> They're telling her to push. "Push! Push harder!" She thinks it's killing her. She's shouting, "How did I get into this?!" I'm coming out now. The doctor says, "It's a boy. A beautiful boy." She's twisting her head back and forth: "I hate him! I hate him! I hate him! Take him away from here! Get rid of him—Now, now!" I'm confused, sad. I don't know what to make out of it, lying there. The doctor's holding me. He says, "Give her something for the pain. It's just the pain. She'll be all right when you give her something."

Ben's rejection by the female and the suggestion of an external substance to ease the situation completed the cycle of traumatic input. He had come to a full understanding of his situation.

His physical prognosis was not good. He had done severe damage to his liver even in the relatively brief period of intense drinking. His heart and arteries were also adversely affected. No amount of understanding could reverse this situation, so I cannot honestly say that he came through therapy restored to his former state of health. The physiological addiction remained. I advised him, as I would any alcoholic, that he must never touch liquor again. Although I couldn't assure his physical well-being for any length of time, he had at least broken the uncontrollable impulse to drink. I could only hope that his new understanding would make it possible for him to abstain.

10

MIGRAINES

HARRISON LASK

HARRISON LASK DECIDED ONE DAY TO GIVE UP EVERYTHING. He left his wife, his nine-month-old son, and his growing optometry practice, telling everyone that he could no longer cope. He did seem aware that these actions constituted some kind of breakdown, and he came to me eagerly when his physician referred him.

At our first interview he described his inability to cope with his work, and particularly with the controls of the State Optical Association. He felt constantly belittled. At home he found himself vying with his baby boy for his wife's affections; he recognized the sickness in this jealousy. The situation seemed complex, but when I asked him what single symptom he would most like to change, he had a simple answer.

"The headaches," he replied.

I looked over my notes. He had not mentioned headaches.

"I have headaches. Every morning. I wake up with them at about dawn. If I take something with caffeine—a cold tablet, or a lot of coffee—it stays under control. Otherwise it becomes a migraine. I vomit; I wrap my head in towels. Nothing helps."

For the sufferer of frequent, regular migraine headaches, life can indeed become intolerable. Living with constant pain has a profound effect on our ability to handle normal everyday situations. Perhaps Harrison's migraines were the source of all of his problems; they were definitely obscuring whatever other problems he had. They had to be attacked. I asked him to describe his headache.

"Let the unconscious mind go back," I told him, "to the period just before waking and, as you're waking, give me the very first thing you're seeing, feeling, thinking . . ."

"I have a headache. I always have a headache. But I've got to get up anyhow. I've got to get up and take something for it."

Using these phrases we discovered the following:

"I have a headache." It's my mother saying it. She must be . . . seven, I think seven months pregnant with me. My father rolls over and says, "You always have a headache. Get up and fix breakfast." She's telling him it's worse. Now she's afraid. She's not supposed to get him up this early. He says, "Well, you've given me a headache for years." She doesn't know what to do. She's getting out of bed and going to the kitchen. Pouring coffee first. She's thinking, "This will make it better."

Recall that the fetus experiences the mother's emotions as its own. Harrison's mother craved caffeine in the morning to cure her headache. Harrison unconsciously took on that pattern, and associated it with domestic instability. This incident is a model for marital alienation, two people failing to cope with each other or their unhappiness.

He moved back from the prenatal period, using the pain in the head as a stimulus. Three similar scenes evolved in rapid succession.

It's dawn. There's something . . . wrong or illegal going on here, I'm not sure what. I'm in the woods, with an Indian girl. We're making love. I think I've done this for a long time . . . every morning or something. . . . I'm very close to her, even though we speak different languages. It's a very close relationship. . . . I'm very wrapped up in what we're doing, but I know there's something wrong. She gasps. There are Indians all around. I can't believe it. So quiet. They've surrounded us. I don't put up a fight. The most decorated one moves toward me. He's dropping a leather thing around my forehead. It has a stick you can twist and tighten. A band of pain, especially in the front, it just gets tighter and tighter. I'm watching my . . . Indian girl. She's resigned, though, she doesn't move. I love her, but it gets mixed up with the pain. This brave tells me . . . he speaks perfect English . . . "This is what happens to men like you . . . who take our women." . . . Tighter and tighter, all I want to do is pass out. Just let me go, let me go. A snap! Snap! My skull. There's just a moment of blinding light. Then nothing. I'm not there anymore.

Now there's a rope around my neck, and the thing around my forehead . . . it's metal. This is different. I'm . . . I'm an Indian, and they're white. There's a metal band around my head that's somehow . . . it's attached to the ropes that have me tied. Every movement I make tightens it. I'm in a crouch . . . there's nothing I can do. This fat man, he says to me, "That's what you get for stealing our buffalo." He and the other men walk away . . . I'm left alone. The buffalo belong to everyone. What does he mean, "their buffalo"? My God, it hurts. There's . . . a whistle. This must be . . . I'm on a railroad track. They've left me on a railroad track. I'm not tied to the tracks . . . but I can't move. Every move just makes my head hurt more. Oh, Christ, here it comes. The cow-catcher . . . the noise . . . I'm thrown in the air. Into the engine . . . head first. . . . I'm floating upward now, there's no pain. I'm not in my body. I can see what's left of the body. It's all below.

Now I'm running. A man is chasing me. I'm fifteen. Still in the woods, running, out of breath. I'm coming through this . . . small stand of trees, and he's there. A man on a horse. He's the one I've been running away from. He got ahead of me. He's very placid. I'm gasping for breath. He's got a shotgun, or rifle or something, but he doesn't seem excited. He says, "I'll teach you to run around with my daughter." The barrel comes up and a white light comes out. There's a roaring in my head. He's shot me in the head. That's all. A roaring. Then nothing.

Aside from the superficial similarity of these scenes, the Indians, the woods, and even the torture bands in the first two, the most significant link here is that all three scenes involve the extreme head pain being accompanied by a "lesson" of some sort. These "lessons" involve love, growing up, and commerce (ownership of the buffalo). In each case, failure to cope with these "lessons" resulted in an excruciating headache and death. Harrison realized this link himself, and said at the end of the session that he had felt the headaches actually "pull away" from him as he experienced the three scenes.

We both knew that these three scenes were crucial. Harrison's inability to cope with the realities of a life in business and marriage was a direct result of the input from these three "lessons." His current headaches were a replay of the headaches caused by punishment long ago. Harrison felt at the end of this session that his headaches were gone forever, but I thought this was overly optimistic. I was hoping for some improvement. What I got instead was an alteration. By the next session Harrison's pain had moved from the morning to the afternoon, and from the front of his head to the back. The headaches had not, however, disappeared as he expected they would. Using his description of these "new" headaches to move Harrison back in time, we soon came upon yet another Indian scene. Harrison was one of two men directly below the chief. He and his rival for the chief's favor were arguing the merits of launching an attack on a nearby white settlement.

The tribe is watching, and I know they sympathize with him. Everyone wants to make war but me. I can see that they are eyeing me . . . suspicious, but I have no choice. I believe it's wrong. I can't participate.

The chief is coming to me now. I'm in a tent, smoking. He says, "Where do you get these ideas . . . to make peace with the white man?" I don't know what to answer him.

It's the same thing over and over again. I just can't do what other people do. He says, "You're probably right. But we must go, that is my decision. It is what my people want." I have to tell him I'm staying here. He nods. We understand . . . we're both doing what we have to do.

The attack took place while Harrison stayed behind, sitting in his tent contemplating. The Indians were routed. The chief did not return. Harrison and his rival were given no choice, by custom, but to fight for the chief's position.

We're on horses. I've heard about this—these challenges. But it's different than being in battle. We're sizing each other up. I feel ambivalent about this. He's charging at me, slashing at me, past me . . . I'm off balance now, but I stay mounted. . . . I feel blood running into my eye. He's slashed my head open . . . across the forehead, I guess. I can picture what it must look like but I can't see it. I can just feel the blood. He's coming again now. He'll kill me. He'll kill me. These things happen so fast. I see the chance. I don't know how I know to do it, but I've leapt off the horse—leapt right at him. Knock him over backwards. Both of us on the ground now. There's a rock in my hand. One I stumbled on. I just found it in my hand. I'm hitting him. Over and over. He's not fighting back now. I've killed him. It's all so fleeting. I didn't know what I was doing. I just killed him. Like an animal. But he's not dead yet. He's sort of half dead. It's very . . . mysterious. He looks up at me without malice . . . again, he knows that this is part of what we must do . . . tribal custom . . . the way we have always lived. I don't think I can stand it.

Harrison's description of the tribal situation brought to mind his difficulties with the State Optical Association, which was, I knew, a clubby group with an elaborate social structure to accompany its code of ethics.

The burial ritual is beginning now. . . . Someone has brought me a cool leaf—a broad, wet green leaf to put on my head. I can hear the drumming. I'm sitting on a rock by the river, thinking how I am going to talk to them. As a preacher of peace who has just committed murder. What can I possibly tell them? Mmh . . . A rock or . . . I'm falling . . . the world's spinning . . . someone hit me from behind, on the back of the head with a rock, or . . . I don't know what . . . the pain . . . the pain. I've fallen in the river. It's his supporters . . . two of them. I can see them as I go in. I'm going to drown now, I know it.

I can see the moonlight hit the water and break up on the ripples. My mouth is full of water . . . I'm drowning now. All I'm aware of is the light, the water, and the pain. My head hurts.

These three symptoms took Harrison to his birth into this life.

The light . . . it's a flashlight . . . the doctor's got it inside. . . . I can feel the pressure on all sides. . . . He's saying, "It looks like his head's in the right place. Dammit, he's getting stuck in there."

Harrison described the insertion of a metal retractor, which struck him at the base of his skull. The sudden cold impact shot through him.

It's like a shiver runs through me, but I don't think I'm actually shaking . . . it just feels like the same thing. He's got this metal thing against my head . . . and he's saying, "He's stuck . . . what'd I tell you." Now he's putting his finger in my mouth . . . I'm suffocating . . . or drowning. He's pulling. Pulling . . . and I'm out. The light's glaring everywhere. I'm . . . I think I'm starting to breathe now. It's very confusing . . . it's a relief, though.

The finger in the mouth, the flashlight, and the cold metal striking Harrison's skull from behind mirrored his death in the river. Before Harrison returned to full consciousness, he said, as he had at his first session, that he felt the pain in his head recede, and that a new "clarity" seemed to come over him. By the time of his third session his headaches had become bi-weekly, and by the fourth they were gone entirely.

Harrison's headaches were the only symptom we attacked during the course of his therapy. He remained unwilling to cope with highly organized groups. He resigned from the State Optical Association and could never return to his optometry practice. He preferred to live the way he was rather than ferret out every symptom in his behavior pattern. His marriage concerned him far more than his career, and the absence of head pain allowed him to concentrate on putting it back in shape.

Past Lives Therapy, as I have said before, is oriented toward eliminating specific symptoms one at a time. I have had patients return to me long after initial treatment, ready to work on some aspect of their behavior that had been ignored or unrecognized during the initial work. I would not be surprised to see Harrison Lask back in my office one day, but perhaps I will not. If he is able to lead a satisfying life without changing his behavioral patterns then it is his responsibility to himself to do so.

11

HYPERACTIVITY

CHUCK JAMES

SOCIETY SEES THE HYPERACTIVE CHILD AS AN UNFORTUNATE nuisance. This disorder affects children from preschool age through adolescence, and occasionally beyond. Victims are fidgety, unable to concentrate, unable to absorb knowledge at a normal rate, and in a state of constant movement. Very little is done for them, apart from administration of drugs to keep them "calm." These drugs, I suspect, are more helpful to the people surrounding the hyperactive child than to the child himself.

The first problem we encounter with such children in Past Lives Therapy is eliminating drug usage. Drugs keep the unconscious mind at an unreachable distance. By the time Chuck James arrived at my office for his second appointment he had been off all drugs for a week, and I had done my best to remove loose papers, breakable ashtrays, and other small items of all sorts from the surrounding area. Chuck, eleven years old, redheaded, so skinny he looked like he was put together with wires, still managed to knock over his chair and pull the notes I had made from his first session onto the floor.

"Look, Doctor," his mother cried. "I'll never be able to control him without drugs."

There was defiant triumph in Mrs. James' voice. She harbored a lot of hostility for her son. Part of her insistence upon feeding him pills came from her own need to prove to him that he was an inadequate child, one who could never get along as normal children did. Naturally the picture of

the relationship between mother and son did not come solely
from her one comment; I knew something of the history of
the pregnancy and of Mrs. James' marriage. I was sure that
a good number of Chuck's problems began in a rather tumultuous prenatal period. Mrs. James was seventeen and single
when Chuck was conceived. Her short-lived marriage to
Chuck's father had been constantly tense, frequently marred
by emotional confrontations. The couple lived with Mrs.
James' mother, who intensely disliked her daughter's new
husband for "what he did to her." Nonetheless, she would
not allow Mrs. James to have an abortion. This kind of
highly charged situation is bound to affect a developing
fetus. Once Chuck became calm enough to begin his session,
the first images he arrived at were prenatal. In talking about
his homelife, Chuck always returned to the phrase, "I wish
they would just leave me alone." We used this as our starting
point.

> "Just let me alone . . . just let me alone. . . ." My
> mother's saying it . . . I'm a very little baby. I'm not
> really a baby yet . . . I see gray all around me . . . I'm
> inside still. I'm three months along . . . my mother is
> saying, "Let me alone, just let me alone."

Chuck repeated the phrase over and over, his voice raised
in panic, and he began to cry.
"What's happening?" I asked.

> Mom's crying. Grandma's standing over her, looking down
> at her. Grandma's saying, "You have to do something. You
> can't be calm and let this happen." . . . I guess she's just
> found out I'm . . . going to be born. . . . Everyone's very
> upset . . . Grandma's saying, "How can you be so calm?
> There's nothing to be calm about!"

This is the first of Chuck's prenatal memories: a concrete
order not to be calm. Following this comment, Chuck played
back the following dialogue between his mother and his
grandmother:

MOTHER: I don't know what to do. I'm so confused—just leave me alone.

GRANDMOTHER: Well, you've *got* to take this medication.

MOTHER: All these pills make me sick. I want an abortion. I can't stand it any longer. This baby'll drive me crazy!

Mrs. James had learned from her own mother to use drugs as an expression of hostility. She could only treat her son as she'd been treated. This was Chuck's first encounter with drugs in his current life. He equated them with punishment, with wrongdoing.

It's later now . . . I'm still inside my mother, but it's later. My father is there. He's tickling Mother. He's holding her down and tickling her all over. She hates it. She's screaming, "Stop! Stop!" She's out of control. It's laughter . . . but it's panic . . . I can't stand it! I mean . . . she can't stand it . . . we're . . . it's all the same . . . her and me . . . we're churning around, very crazy, all hysterical and shaking. . . .

Chuck had begun to pull and tear at the fabric of the couch he was lying on as he described this scene. His knees were pulled up toward his chest, and he kicked his feet spasmodically as he described this incident. It took more than the normal number of repetitions to detach him; we continued to go over and over the incident until his physical movements became normal again. But, as he lay on the couch, breathing softly, he became tensed, the muscles tightening in his face.

"Where are you?" I asked.

"In a schoolyard," he replied.

Chuck was a complete anarchist in the classroom, where punishment had become an everyday experience. School was one of his major traumas.

I'm still inside Mother. She's trying to finish school . . . but it's too hard. Everyone makes fun of her because I'm inside. She's sick all the time . . . thinking, "I've got to get out of here." She wants to fight her way out. That's what she's saying, but I feel like I want to fight my way out when she says it. I want to fight my way out . . . I'm . . . not there anymore. I'm in a cell. Like a jail cell. I'm a prisoner.

This was the first past life Chuck encountered. He was held in a jail for having murdered his own infant son. The time seemed to be the 1940s, somewhere in America.

I don't know what I'm waiting for . . . I've got to get out of here. They're going to come get me. Someone at the door. "It's time, let's go." I'm fighting with them. They're dragging me down a long hall. It's dark . . . damp. I can hear water dripping somewhere, and I'm starting to kick and scream. I'm all numb outside—I can't even feel them touching me. They're strapping me into a chair. It's the electric chair. I'm fighting, kicking, screaming, but it's no use. I know what's going to happen. I'm alone in this room. A sudden burst like white lights, but in my head. . . . My body's bouncing in the chair against the straps . . . shaking, like vibrating . . . my mind's jumping. It's the shock . . . the electricity. Then—one great flashing light. And it stops. The current is off. A man is coming in . . . putting his head to my chest . . . says, "He's an active one . . . he's not dead yet." He's talking about me. There's another burst inside my head. They turned it on again.

At this point Chuck clenched his jaws shut and shook for a moment or two. Then he relaxed.

"I'm dead," he reported.

Chuck had isolated a past-life incident and the prenatal scene that had restimulated it. His mother's aggressive fear, her sense of entrapment in the classroom, had played back Chuck's similar emotions as he awaited electrocution in the past. School, itself, was the trigger for these emotions. His feelings in the classroom were those of a crazed convict on death row; his behavior was that of a man suffering electrical shocks. Chuck lived his life as an alternating cycle: periods of belligerent waiting, followed by bursts of uncontrolled physical action—his equivalent of electrocution. He felt guilty about his inability to control himself, and shamed by his mother, who was forever having to "explain" about him. This guilt was linked to a different type of electrical shock.

I'm in a field, I'm just a kid . . . like me, the way I am now, but younger, even. I'm barefoot. There's dew on the grass . . . this high grass, and I can feel the cuffs of my pants getting wet. I'm just wandering around . . . it's such a nice day. . . . My father's driving a wagon across the field. He's not paying much attention, but he waves. I'm running toward him, toward him through the grass. There's a wire fence between us and I'm reaching for it. There's a big jolt. This fence, it must be electric. I'm stuck . . . I can't get off of it. I'm screaming, and I'm . . . jittering . . . my mother's screaming too, I can see her running toward me, shouting. Even while this current is going through me I can hear her. She's saying, "I told you to watch him! You've killed your own son with that damn wire!" He's shouting, "Don't touch him! Don't touch him!" He's pushing at me with a stick, trying to knock me off the wire. She's hysterical, screaming and jumping. He's pushing me. Pushing me to the ground.

Chuck was left alive, but severely brain damaged. Although he was able to comprehend what was going on around him, his parents were unaware of this capability. They fought openly in his presence, and discussed him as if he were deaf. As he looked on helplessly their relationship slowly collapsed in an atmosphere of bitterness and recrimination, for which he felt responsible.

Many of Chuck's prenatal incidents encompassed the same emotions. Since his mother and father married *only* because he was conceived, and since the marriage put both of them through hell, he was born carrying the burden of overwhelming guilt. Because of this, we moved between the prenatal and this second electrocution many times before finally reaching a total detachment. We did not reach his birth until our final session.

> On the table. She's lying there, and I'm thinking, "I want out of here." I'm kicking like crazy. The doctor's saying, "Very active," and there's a nurse. She says, "Better active than the other way." Mother's screaming. They keep saying, "Get control of yourself. Keep in control." She's shaking. Her whole body's just got the shakes . . . like hysterical . . . they're giving her a shot. Now I can see light. It's cold. Bright shining light. The doctor is pulling on me. She's still out of control. They're holding her down. Just like before. One thing's for sure—those shots don't do any good.

From the end of this session, Chuck neither took nor needed any medication to control his hyperactivity.

It is impossible to predict how quickly the effects of therapy will be felt. Although I rarely see a patient for more than three months, I sometimes see one for only a few weeks. In cases like Chuck's where the traumatic events are centered heavily in a very few incidents and the prenatal period, improvement will usually be rapid and steady. Moreover, work with children tends to be especially satisfactory; they have not been trained by society to reject reincarnation, and are more receptive to the technique.

12

INCIPIENT CANCER

KAY FOLGER

KAY FOLGER FACED ONE OF THE MOST DIFFICULT, POTENTIALLY tragic situations any patient of mine has dealt with. She was twenty-four years old, engaged to be married, and looking forward to life as a wife and mother, when she was informed that her Pap test indicated incipient cervical cancer (class 4). Her gynecologist pressed for a complete hysterectomy —which would, of course, prevent Kay from ever having children and might also severely damage her sexual outlook. It was not an ideal way to begin a marriage. Kay was hesitant about the operation, and her gynecologist became extremely concerned. She consulted her family physician, who referred her to me.

My beliefs about cancer are considered radical in some circles. I have long felt that cancer is an outgrowth of emotional problems, although I would never claim that the bodily damage done by an existing cancer can be repaired by alleviating those emotional difficulties. In Kay's case there was no sign of actual body deterioration yet, and I believe her experience makes the strongest case for my beliefs about cancer.

As I interviewed Kay, I discovered that her eager anticipation about marriage covered a deep anxiety. She felt guilty about her premarital sexual relationship with her fiancé and fearful of the pain of childbirth. Her self-confidence eroded; she began to be uncertain that she would have the emotional strength or the wisdom to bring up children. As the date of the marriage approached, these instabilities, once rather mild, snowballed and became obsessional. Suddenly she was faced with a physically defective uterus. I was absolutely certain that the emotional and the physical were connected, that Kay's view of marriage was tied to a pattern of stress and injury to her womb, and that her uterus was physically susceptible to cancer because of that stress.

The first incident Kay found was in her prenatal period. The reasons for this should be obvious; her most intimate connection with the uterus was the time she spent inside one. Before she began to work back to her prenatal experiences, she told me that she thought of her mother's marriage as "twenty-five years under stress" and that her father had "never given a damn very much one way or another about the kids." Our first prenatal encounter supports this position completely. We find Kay's mother and father talking during the final month of pregnancy.

> She's saying to him . . . it's kind of more resigned than angry . . . she says, "What I really needed now was another baby. I'm so tired, so worn out all the time. I can't cope with the two I've got . . . ."—and he's not even listening. He says, "Oh, you'll cope somehow, you'll get along. What are you gonna do? Die?"

The phrase, "What I really needed now was another baby" stuck with Kay. A few repetitions triggered the following:

> What I really need is another baby . . . but it's different now . . . it's a man's voice saying it. A man, standing over me. I'm on a bed in a house . . . a stone house . . . and I'm giving birth. There's just three of us—me, my husband, and a midwife. This seems like somewhere in Europe . . . paintings on the wall . . . hunt pictures and things. . . . I'm pushing so hard. He's my husband and he's saying, "What I really needed now was another baby to go along with the ten we've got. Thanks a lot. Eleven years, ten kids. God Almighty."
>
> The midwife is trying to calm him down, and attend to me at the same time, but it's never felt like this before

. . . I just can't do it. I don't know what's happening.
The midwife knows . . . we glance at each other. She
knows I know. Now the baby's coming. . . . She says,
"There's something wrong . . . it isn't acting right . . .
Oh Jesus! The womb is tearing . . . it's tearing open. Oh
Jesus, oh Jesus." I can feel panic and warm . . . something running down around my legs, but I'm beginning
to go now, beginning to pass out. . . . He's saying, "Don't
let her die now, don't let her die," but . . . I can hardly
hear. . . . The midwife says, "My God, look at the womb
. . . it looks like a piece of cheese." I'm out now . . . I
don't know, am I dead? I don't think so . . . not yet . . .
but he's saying, "Her mother said she was too weak. . . .
She never should have married. . . ." I'm leaving the
body now, I'm floating out of it . . . no pain . . . just
moving away. All I'm hearing is, "She never should have
married, she never should have married."

This death binds the concepts of marriage and uterine
destruction. The husband's frantic behavior over the ten
previous children suggested to Kay that childbearing somehow "wears out" the uterus, and this image—the uterus, used
up, worthless—brought Kay into a new life, one in which she
was a male. She was a medical student in eighteenth-century
England, attending an anatomy lecture.

I'm staring at a drawing, a representation of the female
reproductive organs, and this is very strange . . . I can
see, from this vantage point, that it is very primitive . . .
almost completely inaccurate. But from there, I'm believing it . . . I mean . . . I can see myself believing that
that's what the organs look like. . . . I'm male . . . I
don't have any firsthand knowledge. . . . Things were so
different then. . . . They're telling us that the fetus is
conceived as a complete baby . . . that it just gets bigger
and bigger, but never changes shape. And the uterus . . .
seems to be made of lacework, some kind of honeycomb
stuff. . . . It could never carry a baby . . . it just looks
like it's full of little holes.

This description is a variant of the midwife's description of Kay's uterus as looking "like a piece of cheese." A third incident, a scene from the same life, reinforces this image.

I'm watching an autopsy performed by a surgery professor . . . we're dressed in shiny leather aprons . . . more like butchers than doctors, and he's cutting like a butcher. I guess this woman's been dead a long time . . . several days, anyhow. She looks like she was . . . fifty, maybe . . . hard to tell. He's bringing out the womb. . . . Ugh, it's just in ribbons. Just awful . . . she died giving birth. He's saying, "The womb of a mother of seven. The womb is totally destroyed, as it is in most cases where it has been impregnated so often."

As this life progressed we found that Kay resolved to have nothing to do with the reproductive organs, and became an ear, nose, and throat specialist.

With this session we established the link between Kay's concept of the marital state—a situation of constant stress focused in the womb—and her sudden positive cancer test. We had yet to deal with her sexual guilt.

It's cold. I'm tending the fire. All alone. Winter in . . . where? I don't know—it seems to be Montana . . . Wyoming . . . some territory out there. I'm in a cabin, waiting, and I know I'm going to have a baby. It's not showing yet, but I'm only thinking about one thing . . . I don't want to lose this baby. I've lost four already.

My husband's been gone. He's usually gone four days, but now it's almost a week. Almost a week. It's all right, I'm kind of used to it, but this is a special time. I don't want to lose this one, and if he were here . . . I'm all confused. I feel like I should go look for him, but I don't know where to look. Still, the waiting . . . it's killing me. But it'll be dark if I go now. I'm on the porch. It's clear . . . cold. No snow.

There's a . . . kind of a whoop. From the woods. I can feel my abdomen tense. I want to run into the house, but I know what's going to happen. He comes out of the woods . . . Daniel, that's his name. Daniel. He's cut. They've cut . . . patterns in his skin. He's running toward me . . . a stumbling, kind of jerky run across the fields. I've heard about it . . . how the Indians do this . . . this ritualistic . . . carving, but you can't believe it. Like herringbone across his arms and chest. . . . He's going to get here, I can tell. I should run and meet him, but my feet are locked. But he'll make it to me . . . he's calling to me, and he reaches me. He starts to speak. Then I hear it . . . a thud. Against me. He falls against me. There's an arrow in his back. I'm beginning to vomit. I wish . . . oh, I wish I didn't have to do this . . . vomit, now, I wish I could stand it. I can't. I can't.

As Kay described her nausea, I could see her shame, her fear, her humiliation, at not being able to cope with the stress situation. But this was merely the beginning.

There's a brave standing over me. He's waiting for me to be through. A young, very tall Indian. On a horse. He gets down and takes me by the arm. I just want someone to take command, but I'm thinking . . . don't touch me . . . don't hurt the baby. But Daniel's dead . . . who cares about the baby. My head's just spinning, that's all. He takes my arm . . . commanding . . . there doesn't seem to be any brutality in him . . . just leading me into the house.

We're inside. Oh my God, there's only one thing this man can do now. He's got me on the bed, and he's beginning to touch me. To undress me. I don't know, I don't know. I'm . . . just this rushing shame . . . all over my body. He's looking at my body. But he's so gentle. So . . . smooth. I can't . . . there's nothing I can do anyway. No, that's not true . . . I can't help responding. I'm . . . He's exciting me.

Kay described a long, gentle sex act, at the end of which she had a shattering orgasm. Bound up in this physical sensation was an overwhelming sense of guilt and shame that she was having sex with her husband's killer only moments after the murder had occurred. Her feelings, which were confused at the beginning of this episode, when she failed to run to save her husband, have by now been wrung into a tight coil of pleasure/guilt/shame/fear.

He looks down at me, speaking in some tongue I can't understand . . . very smooth tones, but I don't know what he's saying. Finally he gets across to me . . . that this is some kind of tribal thing. It's either him or me. Him or me. There's a knife blade coming at me. At the throat. The throat. So sudden. I can feel the blood running down the neck. Onto my chest. And now my belly. I'm convulsing, contracting, I don't know what I'm doing anymore. Anything . . . just make it over, make it over. . . . He's slit down there. My womb. My fetus. He's got it. I can't be aware of this. I must be dead already. I must be. But there's this one thing. In my mind, or whatever is left there. This feeling . . . it's not exactly a thought. He killed the baby . . . he killed me. Me and the baby.

We could not determine the exact moment of death, but one thing is certain. Kay was left with the lesson that orgasm was irrevocably linked to death, guilt, and damage to the womb.

After this session we worked several fragmentary lives in which Kay had died during pregnancy, and extensively covered one life in which, as an Eskimo woman, she froze to death with an unborn child in her womb. In this life she was able to identify the moment of the fetus's death long after numbness and unconsciousness had overtaken her. She felt enormous guilt in this situation where she was literally frozen, unable to move as her unborn child kicked and complained within her.

In the final life I worked with Kay she never became pregnant at all. She was the second-born twin in a family of twelve. They lived in poverty in Ireland during the infamous potato famine. Kay could recall that her mother had no milk for her, and that she was brought up instead suckling a flour sack soaked in sugar syrup. She was an extremely slow child, and there was some talk in the family that she may have been a bit "touched," a phrase that covered all sorts of mental illness, including retardation. At the age of fourteen she had not menstruated, and her mother became frantic that she might be sterile. Convinced that Kay was "inhabited by the bad spirit," she consulted a priest instead of a doctor.

> I can hear my mother talking to him . . . I'm lying naked under a sheet inside. They're outside. She's saying, "She doesn't have a womb. It's her sin, it's not for us to understand." The priest is telling her something, but he's mumbling. Now they're coming in. It's very dark, and I'm very frightened. I don't even know why, exactly. . . . It's just, I don't understand what she means by sin. I haven't done anything. Nothing that I know about. I'm just under this sheet. He can see me . . . if he looks. He's a young man . . . why can't he be an old man? He's young. In robes, with a . . . a smoke pot he's swinging. Incense . . . and he's talking Latin. She thinks I don't have a womb. Maybe I don't. . . . That's what I'm thinking. What's wrong with me? I feel so ashamed. Why is he looking at me? . . . What's he talking about in Latin? I'm just beginning to cry . . . to cry and cry. . . .

Death in this lifetime occurred many years later, but Kay had never menstruated. She had lived a solitary life within her family's home while the other children got married and moved away. As she lay dying from influenza she heard the following:

> Mother . . . she's an old lady now, she's saying, "Maybe it's best. She was never really right, anyhow. You can't be a full woman without children, that's for sure. You can't have children without a womb. . . ."

Kay's experience in this life recapitulated many of the emotions we had already covered, and added the "advice" in her mother's final words: You can't be a woman without children—you can't have children without a womb. This phrase suggested to me that Kay was in fact "taking care" of her fear of child-rearing by unconsciously generating the destruction of her uterus.

In an attempt to find reinforcement of these emotions, we returned to the prenatal period of this lifetime. The eighth month of pregnancy found Kay's father offering the following solution to his wife's fertility:

"Why don't you just have him cut it out when the baby's born? Cut the whole uterus out. . . . Didn't I read that somewhere?" Mother is . . . I can feel her muscles contract just from the suggestion. . . . She says, "What a thing to say . . . a woman's womb is the most important thing to her. I'm not going to mutilate myself just so you can have fun!" He's furious at her, but she . . . she's kind of good in these situations . . . she's watching him walk out of the room. Out of the house.

With this argument Kay's mother reiterated the philosophy that an Irish mother long ago had introduced: The womb is the most important thing to a woman—a woman is incomplete without a womb. Kay reported that in her preliminary meetings with her gynecologist about the cancer test he had been very direct on this issue.

He said to me, "I hope you're not one of those women who think that childbearing is everything. That you can't be a 'whole woman' without bearing children. That's nonsense, you know." I had a terrible reaction when he said it. I guess he was trying to prepare me. I got very violent.

Everything Kay's gynecologist suggested was, of course, in direct opposition to Kay's "training" through several lives. Her violent reaction fit perfectly into the patterns we had uncovered. A final session with Kay brought forth these two brief scenes in the third and fourth months of the prenatal period.

Mother's sitting in a chair, and she's thinking, "Poor

Ellen, she has cancer. . . ." Ellen was an aunt of mine
. . . she died. She must have been alive here. "She has
cancer. I wonder if they got it in time. I'd hate to lose a
breast that way . . . but I wonder if I have cancer. Maybe
I'm pregnant . . . I hope so, God knows. I should have a
test . . . but I'm afraid to find out. I wonder. I wonder
if the uterus is more susceptible than the breast. I just
don't want to know. . . ." She's rocking in a chair . . .
and it's raining out.

A month later Kay's parents were at dinner, Kay recalled:

She's eating, and she's very . . . nervous, waiting to say
something, waiting for the right moment . . . trying to
make it a positive statement. . . . It's very nerve-wracking
. . . my father's just eating. . . . She's thinking, "I wish
he'd look up from that damn paper." He never does.
Finally she just says it: "Well, I guess I don't have cancer
. . . the doctor says I'm pregnant." She doesn't know what
he'll say. She's just stopped. He says, "Thanks a lot. That's
just what we needed—another baby."

With this statement we had come full circle on Kay Folger.
The phrase that had begun her therapy also ended it. She
returned to the gynecologist and was again tested for uterine
cancer. All tests were negative. The wedding took place on
schedule. Within two years she had given birth to a healthy
baby boy.

The improvement in Kay's emotional state was steady and
swift enough to justify holding off on immediate surgery.
Of course in treating incipient cancer, we are, in some sense,
playing with fire. If a patient failed to improve, or had difficulty finding the link between his cancer and the emotional
component causing it, medical treatment would become
necessary.

Kay's case is uncommon, but I believe it points to an un-
explored area for research in the prevention and treatment
of a disease that is rapidly becoming an international obsession.

III

LIFE
CYCLES

IN A DECADE OF WORK WITH PAST LIVES THERAPY, I HAVE
been able to form few generalizations. Each patient is unique,
each problem individual. Every life has its crucial events,
the isolated moments when controlling patterns are introduced. One general rule holds true: The bulk of therapy is
concentrated in three special phases of the life cycle—the
prenatal period, birth, and death. The great majority of
past-life incidents I encounter are set in one of these three
areas. In this section I have devoted a chapter to each experience. Each invites a particular kind of trauma, each has
a particular significance in the complete life cycle.

The concluding chapter deals with an area I have chosen
to set apart from my other casework, the space between lives.

This "void," where the unconscious mind waits to choose a
new body, can be seen as the end of the life cycle or as the
beginning. It has a powerful lure to many people. Sadly, I
have found it less useful in therapy than I might have hoped.
I will explore the reasons for its limited value, and a case
where its exploration *has* been productive, in the final chapter of "Life Cycles."

13

LIFE IN THE WOMB

IF REINCARNATION TAKES PLACE, EACH LIFE IS NO MORE THAN a single cycle in an endless pattern. Our lives are like a series of journeys, and each journey begins in the womb. Any mother who has ever been awakened by a kicking fetus can confirm that there is physical life before birth. In Past Lives Therapy we discover that the fetus is capable of unconscious perception as well—an awareness of everything that is happening around it.

This life inside the womb is shrouded in mystery, as if a veil had been drawn over our prenatal awareness at birth. Inside the uterus there is no conscious mind present, and the entrance of the conscious mind, at birth, seems to close off access to the unconscious. In Past Lives Therapy we reach back to this crucial nine months, and there we find the roots of every patient's behavior.

Among the many things that make this prenatal period unique to the life cycle, perhaps the foremost is this: It is the only prolonged time when the unconscious mind functions alone, unaided by consciousness. Earlier I compared the unconscious to a tape recorder, indiscriminately recording everything, and storing the information without interpreting it. In effect, the fetus records all of the mother's thoughts, everything said to the mother, by her, and in her presence, as if it applied to him.

The unborn child, awaiting the beginning of conscious life, is profoundly affected by this prenatal awareness. With no conscious mind to discern or interpret, the unconscious plays back any past-life incidents triggered by events in the mother's life. These incidents shape the behavior patterns of the child. At birth the infant will begin a life of trying to resolve those past-life events without ever knowing what they are.

Because the life patterns are determined in the womb, it is essential for a patient to cover the events of his conception and fetal development in detail. Any past life he encounters *must* be related to an incident in his prenatal period of his present life. We cannot detach a patient from the past life without also detaching him from the fetal incident that "triggered" his unconscious memory of it. Because of this, almost every therapy session includes work in the prenatal.

There are four separate, distinct phases of the prenatal period: the moment of conception, the period of time when the mother begins to suspect she is pregnant, the moment of confirmation, and the remaining time before birth. Each phase is subject to its own particular type of trauma and stress. A patient will rarely deal with them in that order, however. Generally speaking, I will allow a patient to go through the sequence of past-life incidents that seem to be linked by a similar trauma, and then ask him to move into the prenatal and find the event or phrase that triggered those past-life memories. I am never sure where the patient will lead me, but usually, by the time therapy is complete, we will have encountered trauma in all four phases of fetal development.

From time to time I find myself involved with a patient who is extremely reluctant to move into the prenatal period. This reticence usually indicates that something out of the ordinary lurks there. When this occurs it is doubly important that we uncover what seeks to remain well hidden.

For Janice Hallister there was an immediate block. She came to me complaining of a variety of problems—headaches, spastic colon, insomnia—but all of her difficulties seemed to culminate in violent temper tantrums. These periods of irrational anger seemed to imply more than simple dissatisfaction with her life; they were followed by the feeling of a complete void closing in on Janice. Sometimes she stayed

in bed with the shades drawn for as long as two days following a tantrum.

The tantrums were brought on by different events, and
Janice admitted that at times she lashed out at garage mechanics, salespersons, and other people of no importance to
her. But her outbursts were most frequently directed at the
men in her life. As a result, she could not maintain a relationship for any length of time. She found her boyfriends
either too dependent on her or too demanding that she be
dependent on them. These situations invariably led to open
hostility for Janice; one after another, her romantic attachments exploded.

Several things Janice said in her initial interview indicated
heavy identification with her mother in the prenatal period.
She described her involvement in psychoanalysis as "a long,
hard road." She also told me that after her mother's death
she had elected to travel the three thousand miles home by
bus, even though she could easily have afforded the plane
fare. Again she had chosen the long, arduous path. I felt that
the nine months in the womb were probably the first long,
hard road in this life, and when she flatly refused to explore
this area of her life, I knew I was right.

We found several past lives in which Janice was a twin;
in one she was a Siamese twin, battling for dominant position in the womb. In each of these past lives there was an
identity struggle, but no sign of tantrums. Janice replayed
these struggles in her current relationships with men, but
since she would not explore the prenatal, it was impossible
to fully erase the past-life memory. Our first attempts to
reach the prenatal covered her conception, but she was unwilling to move forward. She had described a death in battle.
We had identified World War II as the time period and I
knew that the conception following this death would be conception into the present life.

JANICE HALLISTER: I hear screaming, and the sounds of artil-
lery. Explosions, people yelling. I'm not there anymore,

though, I'm moving someplace, someplace where I hear
similar sounds.

DR. NETHERTON: What are you aware of as you move into
that? What do you hear that's familiar?

JANICE: It's all black, wet . . . my parents' voices. But I
don't want to tell you anything. I won't go in there.
Don't push me. There's nothing here to talk about.
Don't make me go in the uterus.

From this I knew only that Janice was conceived in circumstances somehow related to battle. We tried several other
ways of entering the uterus, but could not get by her block.
Each time we approached, I was greeted with the same
phrases, quoted above. I realized that these phrases must
themselves be part of the prenatal trauma. I decided to look
for the phrases in infancy or early childhood, hoping to back-
track into the prenatal period.

DR. NETHERTON: All right. Go to a time in this life, somewhere in your childhood, and see if you can find the
phrase, "I don't want to go in there, don't make me" or
"Don't push me, I won't go in there." Where are you?

JANICE: I'm two years old. My parents are talking. My
mother's saying, "Goddamnit, go without me. I'll keep
the baby, and you go!" But my father's taunting her.
"I want you to go too, it's more fun that way. It's only
a fun house." She says, "Don't give me that, the last time
I went I had a horrible time. I won't go in that place.
Fun house! It's a horrible, scary place. I'm warning you,
don't push me."

DR. NETHERTON: Now, what comes to mind when you think
of those same phrases in the prenatal? Inside mother,
when she's saying, "I won't go in there, don't push me."

JANICE: There's lots of noise. She's shaking, looking in the
opening of a fun house, and that's just what she's saying
—"Don't push me." She's thinking, "Goddamnit, why
am I letting him push me? It's obvious he doesn't care
about my feelings. Why don't I just kick him out? He
can't do this to me. It's hot. I can't breathe in here."

DR. NETHERTON: Does Mother knew she's pregnant?
JANICE: I don't think so. She's not thinking about it. I can
    feel the walls around me tensing. She's screaming.
    Father's saying, "You love it, you know you love it!"
    She's hit him. She's really scared, that's all I know.

Once we'd broken the barrier into the prenatal, Janice had
no difficulty returning there. The phrase "I won't go in
there" acted as a shut-off command. It effectively blocked
access to the womb. This is a prime example of the tape
recorder quality I have described.

Janice's past lives paled in comparison to the trauma of the
prenatal period. We went back to the World War II battlefield (where Janice had been male) and again covered her
conception.

It's all black and wet. I'm not inside yet. I don't know
    where I am. They're making love, but they're fighting . . .
    he's cursing at her: "Lie still, you filthy slut." It's like lan-
    guage you never hear, like language out of a book. She's
    shouting at him, "Take that thing out of me, you bastard,
    get away from me." I don't understand this. She's biting
    him, and . . . Oh, my God, I'm here. I'm inside. In the
    womb. It's quivering. She's shouting, "I can't help it, I
    can't help it. Goddamn you, I hate you. I hate you, I hate
    you!"
    Everything's gone black. I can't . . . I seem to be lost.
    Completely lost. She's not there anymore. I feel like we
    died. I can hear my father saying, "Come back, come back
    here with me. Are you all right? Are you crazy or some-
    thing?" Now we're coming back. I can feel her moving.
    She's in the john, on the toilet. Thinking . . . "I wish I
    could get it all out. Flush it all away. I don't know what
    happens to me." There's this terrible feeling of shame with
    her. She's mortified that she responds to sex this way. I
    guess . . . I guess that's how it was.

Janice had left one battle situation and was born into another. (The evidence for this kind of movement from life

to life is further explored in Chapter 16, "The Space Between Lives." For the purposes of examining the prenatal
period, it is sufficient to report that this is what Janice recalled.) Her parents, it developed, lived in a sadomasochistic
relationship, in which they constantly punished each other.
Time and time again we encountered these "make-believe"
fights, which climaxed in sexual intercourse. Janice's mother
was obviously powerless to control her instincts in this direction, but the aftermath of such sessions left her with a feeling
of low self-esteem and loneliness. As for the "blackout period" immediately following orgasm, that was not explained
until a later incident—the moment when the pregnancy was
confirmed.

> In a doctor's office. The walls are rigid. I know some-
> thing's wrong. The doctor's yelling at my mother. There's
> been a lot of yelling. He's saying, "There's nothing you
> can do about it," and she's screaming at him, "Don't tell
> me that! I don't want to hear it! I don't need that from
> you!" She's out of control. Just like me. This is how I get.
> He's just as angry, though. He says, "Look. You're going
> to have a baby. There's nothing you can do about it, so just
> sit down, shut up, and cool off." I hear a door slamming.
> Now she's picked up something and she's throwing it.
> There's a crash. She's thrown something against the wall.
> Now she's going away again. I feel it . . . that disappear-
> ance. Like we're dying. I'm terrified, like spinning in
> circles. Dizzy . . . I can hear the doctor's voice. . . . He's
> saying, "My God, she's an epileptic into the bargain."
> We're out. Blackness.

With this session I felt we had reached an explanation of
the long "dead" periods Janice felt after her own tantrums
—the days in bed with the phone off the hook and the shades
drawn. The rejection voiced by her mother was reinforced
by the mother's "disappearance" as the seizure took effect.
All of this was tied to violent temper. Each time Janice found
herself in a situation where dependence was an issue, where
behavior as a couple became an important topic, she went

into physical fits. Despite the fact that she was not an epileptic, her behavior followed epileptic patterns.

A final event loomed large in Janice's prenatal period—an argument between her mother and her grandmother sometime in the seventh month of pregnancy.

> I can feel Mother's frustration. She's taking it out on me
> . . . I mean, I'm feeling the cramps, the tightness, that
> terror that comes over me when I know I'll explode. I guess
> it's *her* feelings that *I'm* experiencing . . . I can't tell. It
> seems like she's playing the child to her own mother here
> . . . I'm sorry . . . I'm very confused. I'm a child, and
> she's my mother, but she's a child yelling at her own
> mother. She's saying. "You'll just have to accept it. You
> can talk to the doctor if you don't believe me." Grandma's
> shouting at her, "I won't accept it. I don't accept it. You
> never tell me anything except what'll hurt me most. You're
> making this up. I know it. I know your ways . . ." and
> Mother's shouting, "I do have fits, I do have fits! God-
> damnit, listen to me." She's pounding on the table. Now
> Grandma's screaming at the same time. "Don't have your
> temper fits with me. You little bitch, go scream at that
> lousy man of yours."

With this sentence we hit squarely on Janice's problem. Unconsciously, she was taking her grandmother's advice to her mother. We still had a traumatic birth to cover, but I knew that the prenatal period, with its fits, tantrums, violent sex, and finally this infuriated suggestion that venting anger at men, or at a mate, was somehow the proper solution to things, was the crux of Janice's problem. This is not to say that Janice's therapy was without reference to her past lives. We arrived at almost every prenatal incident from some point in the past. But invariably the events in the prenatal period had a more direct bearing on Janice's present life than did her past-life traumas. While this is not common, it illustrates the essential importance of the prenatal period in every case. It is the longest time period in our lives when the unconscious mind reigns supreme, without a conscious mind to analyze or act as a filter. In this embryonic space the rules of the game, so to speak, are set up for us. The issues that will confront us throughout conscious life are introduced, and the "memory" of certain past-life traumas is locked into position. Then, just as this preamble is fully assembled, it is made inaccessible by the entrance of the conscious mind, at birth.

14

THE EXPERIENCE OF BIRTH

IT IS BY NO MEANS RADICAL TO SUGGEST THAT THE BIRTH trauma greatly affects our lives. The birth trauma is much dealt with in psychology texts and popular works on human behavior. My experience in Past Lives Therapy adds a single significant factor to what others have already said on the subject; the trauma of birth is deeply interwoven with trauma in past lives and in the prenatal period immediately preceding birth.

The factor of human behavior most controlled by the birth experience is the ability to handle stress. Birth is the first conscious stress experience we have. The mother usually finds giving birth the most heavily stressed experience of her life. Our reaction to stress throughout our lives is naturally related to this first massive dose of it. If the mother meets the situation with a strong will and with deep love for the infant being born, and if the doctors, nurses, and the father (when present) handle the situation with calm and confidence, the child will, in all likelihood, bring those positive attributes to bear in his own dealings with future stress. If, on the other hand, the birth situation is complicated, and is dealt with by panic, drug use, and rejection of the infant, stress will be a lifelong problem for that child, as it has been for a young woman named Delia Hall.

Delia had no mechanisms whatever for handling stress. She was twenty years old, but behaved like a child. Because she was prone to sudden bursts of anger, tears, headaches, muscle spasms, and other disorders common to victims of stress, her doctor had put her on six separate medications, including an antacid, tranquilizers, and pain-killers, which she took every day. Delia knew that this was not a healthy pattern of behavior; she came to me to find the source of her inability to function. She characterized her problem in one phrase: impending doom. She felt death lurking around every corner, catastrophe awaiting her each morning. She could not face the day without her morning pills, could not face the night without her evening pills. She was totally dominated by whatever man she was dating at the time, and was drawn to men who, she said, "don't ask me to make any decisions, even when I hate the decisions they make for me."

When she was not being pushed around by men, Delia was under the thumb of a mother who had used the pregnancy and birth of her daughter as an excuse for behaving like a martyr. The pregnancy had been a mistake; Delia was conceived immediately upon her father's return from prison, where he had been for more than a year. The mother had been warned not to have any more children after her previous child had been born dead. She suffered a tipped uterus and her pelvic area had been damaged by an earlier accident. Needless to say, the period of pregnancy was anything but placid.

Delia's past lives were replete with scenes of torture at the hands of men. She found multiple scenes of sex abuse and torture, often leading to death. At the moment of death she frequently heard a man saying, "Now you've killed her," or "That'll kill her," or some variation thereof. These phrases were triggered in the prenatal period by Mrs. Hall's husband and her doctor begging her to abort the fetus: "It'll kill you," "It could kill you," "You might die." Mrs. Hall rejected the idea of the abortion, but became heavily dependent on tranquilizers to calm her worries about the approaching date of delivery.

The obstetrician anticipated that Delia's birth would be abnormal. He delivered her in an operating room equipped with high seating so that other doctors and medical students could observe the work. For some reason the doctor declined to perform a Cesarean section, despite Mrs. Hall's tipped uterus, and Delia's birth became risky. At her sixth session, after a long working of the prenatal period, we finally established the scene of delivery. What follows is an edited transcript of Delia's first encounter with stress in this life, as she related it to me.

DR. NETHERTON: Now I'd like you to move into the scene of your birth. What do you see, hear, think, feel?

DELLA: Oh my God! Not now, I'm not ready, it's not time . . .

DR. NETHERTON: Who's saying that?

DELIA: Mother. Oh, pain, I feel pain . . .

DR. NETHERTON: Is Mother in labor?

DELIA: Yes. They're taking her to the hospital. "Do something. . . . Save my baby. Give me something . . . I can't stand the pain." Screaming . . . panicked . . .

DR. NETHERTON: Is Mother at the hospital now?

DELIA: I don't know . . . I scc white . . . a woman in white standing over Mother . . . a needle. . . . She says, "This will make it easier for you. Just relax."

DR. NETHERTON: What are you aware of now?

DELIA: Mother's moving away from me . . . she's relaxing . . . I feel frightened. It's like she's leaving . . . like she's dying and leaving me alone . . . now of all times! This is when I need her help most.

DR. NETHERTON: At birth?

DELIA: Yes. I'm frightened.

DR. NETHERTON: What's happening now?

DELIA: Someone's saying, "Give her another injection, keep her calm. If we don't keep her under she'll cause real problems."

DR. NETHERTON: What's happening with Mother that the doctor wants to give her an injection?

DELIA: I feel a kind of turbulence. She's moving around.

DR. NETHERTON: What's happening now?

DELIA: I feel a needle in my arm . . . her arm, I guess. I'm
feeling calmer now, dull . . . frightened. Mother's going away again. I don't know how I can do this alone.

DR. NETHERTON: Where's Mother now?

DELIA: On a table in a white room. She's looking up at white,
everywhere. The doctor's saying, "Put her under further,
we don't want any more problems. There's another shot,
and now I feel like I can't get out. Like there's a . . . this
. . . something holding me down, holding Mother
down, this groggy fear . . . we'll never survive it. I
guess it's all these drugs. I feel numb, and I think she's
going to die. One doctor's practically screaming: "You
should have done a Cesarean, but now it's too late for
that! You'll never deliver this baby alive!"

    Now they're fighting with each other. The other one
says, "Of course I will, I'll turn the baby around the
placenta." The first one says, "Well, that's fine. That'll
kill it for sure. You'll probably kill them both." I'm
down here all alone. I'm stuck, there's nothing I can do.

This dialogue reinforced a sense of stress leading to doom;
at the same time, it triggered several past-life deaths by torture, where the phrases "You killed her," and "That'll kill
her for sure" had been followed by actual death. A further
replay of the torture scenes was still to come.

DELIA: I feel pressure . . . someone's pushing on Mother's
stomach. She seems dead to me. Now a stabbing pain,
cold, I guess it's just cold, it feels like a stab. Some cold
metal, a clamp—on my left shoulder. I'm straining
against something, someone's saying, "You'll never get
that baby around the placenta." Now there's tremendous
pressure . . . my head and shoulder—my neck—someone's pushing, pulling, one of them says, "Be careful
now, you're going to kill it."

DR. NETHERTON: Who's saying that?

DELIA: That first doctor. The other one says. "Get out of the
way . . . everything's fine."

DR. NETHERTON: What's happening now?

DELLA: "It's stuck. Won't go any farther."

DR. NETHERTON: Is the doctor saying that?

DELIA: Yes. I feel stuck. Frightened. "You'll never do this. It'll die before you get it out. Hold this, I'm going to push."

DR. NETHERTON: Is that more conversation between the doctors?

DELIA: Yes. I feel something cold and metallic on my butt. It's pushing my butt, and something warmer, a hand maybe, is pulling on my right shoulder. "My God, that must hurt."

DR. NETHERTON: Who's saying that?

DELIA: One of the doctors. "Be careful! Be careful!" Someone's shouting. Commotion. "It'll get stuck! It'll get stuck! You'll never get it out. You'll never get it out!" Now something's pushing the left side of my butt. Pulling my left shoulder. "Put her under further, she's resisting too much."

DR. NETHERTON: Who's saying that?

DELIA: The doctor's saying that about my mother. He's giving her another injection. Force on my head . . . a hand, it's cramped, crowded in here. I'm being forced to turn. . . . It's very hard for my head and shoulders to turn the way they're being pushed . . .

DR. NETHERTON: What words are you hearing as all of this is happening?

DELIA: "It's stuck again . . . goddamn it." "It's impossible, that baby has got to be dead by now." "After all this trouble I'll get it out one way or another . . ."

DR. NETHERTON: Is this another dialogue between the doctors?

DELIA: Yes. Something's pulling me down now. . . . My head gives and drops down. . . . "The head's down. Get the forceps . . ."

DR. NETHERTON: What's the mother feeling as the doctor says this?

DELIA: She's moaning. "Don't let her come out of it. Keep her under."

DR. NETHERTON: What's the doctor doing now?

DELIA: Another injection. I feel numb again. Panicky. I'm beginning to see light . . . my head's being pulled so I can see light.

DR. NETHERTON: Do you hear any words being said?

DELIA: "It looks like it's dead." The doctor is saying that.

DR. NETHERTON: Where are you as you hear those words?

DELIA: I see light . . . feel sharp stabbing pains in my eyes as the bright light hit, like a migraine. . . . I feel smothering fear, dread . . . I feel drugged. . . . There's another voice . . . "You never know what's going to happen with births like this . . ."

At this point it should be clear where Delia's fear of the unknown future stems from. Her sense of impending doom has been reinforced again and again as she begins to emerge from the womb into the world.

DELIA: It's cold . . . I'm leaving that warm place, moving into the cold. That pain . . . on my shoulder . . . from the cold metal, it's all over me now. It's just the sensation of cold. I've never felt it before. I've been pushed into it, away from Mother . . . I feel all alone. She's not even stirring. I'm all alone here. Someone's saying, "You did it! Congratulations, you didn't kill it after all. I can't believe it, it's alive!" They're walking around with their arms around each other's shoulders. I think. I can't tell. The light's so bright. A blinding pain in my eyes . . . but all so new . . . I can't figure out these sensations, they're all new . . . and no one's paying any attention to me. Oh God!

DR. NETHERTON: What just happened?

DELIA: They've stuck a tube down my throat . . . something's coming up. They're pulling something from my throat. I can't breathe, it's blocked. They're pulling the tube out now, and they put me down again, lay me on a table.

DR. NETHERTON: What's happening to Mother now?

DELIA: She's starting to stir. The doctor says. "Give her one more. She'll be okay, take her to recovery." Mama's going now. The wheels are squeaking on her bed. The doctors are still walking around. They're talking to people up above. There's no one left for me. The nurses are gone. All I hear is, "Congratulations, congratulations." I feel all alone . . . no one's here for me.

This sense of coldness, of solitude, was the final impression of Delia's birth trauma. On reworking the scene we counted the number of drugs given her mother during and immediately following the birth. There were six injections, the precise number of medications it now took Delia to get through her days. Her inability to deal with men except as a passive recipient of their commands grew out of the doctor's impersonal pushing and pulling as she moved down the birth canal. The doctor who delivered Delia saw her birth as a personal triumph for himself, and was only incidentally interested in the baby itself. At the time of her therapy Delia behaved as if this were the only attitude any man could have toward her. Her guilt feelings toward her mother stemmed from the birth complications which almost killed the woman. As a fetus she was extremely responsive to the mood of impending doom in the delivery room, both for herself and for the mother who carried her at great (albeit exaggerated) risk.

Delia's birth is among the most severely traumatic that I have ever encountered. But no birth is without pain, without fear. The infant must face a world populated by doctors and nurses, perfumed with antiseptic, decorated in hard white and chrome. By and large, the people surrounding the birth scene honestly believe that the baby has no perception, and can be disregarded while they go about their work. For the hospital staff it is routine duty; for the mother and father it can be so totally unsettling that they lose track of the infant. The infant's new world will certainly seem to be an unfriendly place where pain is routinely inflicted and fear is not easily comforted. I believe that every person experiences some trauma at birth. But it is the duty of doctors and parents to limit pain and anxiety as much as possible. An awareness of the newborn is essential. He will need holding, touching, reassuring. With the growing popularity of natural childbirth and the Leboyer method of delivery, we can hope that the trauma of birth will be gradually reduced. The result, over a long period of time, will be a population much better equipped to handle stress.

15

THE EXPERIENCE
OF DEATH

SOONER OR LATER EVERY CHILD GETS AROUND TO ASKING THE question: Why must we die? In most cases he will go on asking the question throughout his life. The question has been with us forever, of course; most every philosopher has tangled with it, and every church has formed a good bit of its doctrine trying to answer it. The question will not go away; in our time, death has become the kind of taboo sex was for the Victorians. We don't know what to say to our dying, so we speak to them as if they were in the prime of life. We don't want to look at them, so we create homes where they can be neatly cut off from our "vital" society. We visit them on sufferance. When, at last, they do die, we clean them up with whatever artificial means are available, and weep that they are gone. Something is deeply amiss here. Somehow our own unwillingness to cope with death has led to a senseless, expensive, unfeeling tradition that does little to answer the child's question—Why do we die?—and less to comfort the dying and those who suffer the loss. We are victims of our own death-hysteria.

I have come to see death as a beginning. I still have no answer to the question; I don't know why we die. But our departure from this life is, for me, the moment when we are set free to seek another body. I realize that this attitude will conflict with the religious beliefs of some, and will be thought foolish by others, who are certain that death is the end of everything. But my experience with Past Lives

Therapy has left me with no doubt that we do come back. If death is inexplicable, it is still not to be feared.

I've had only one case where a person came to me knowing she had little time left. Her therapy was an education for both of us. Her name was Grace Hart, and the first words she said in our initial interview were, "I know I've got to die. I just want to do it with some dignity. And as little pain as possible."

Grace had experienced abdominal pain after the collapse of her nineteen-year marriage. The pain was diagnosed as uterine cancer; a hysterectomy was performed. But, within months, the cancer reappeared elsewhere in her body. There was no chance for recovery. She entered therapy with full knowledge of her condition. Her doctor had referred her to me because she asked for "any available means" of emotionally handling her illness. I explained the scope of the therapy and its limited claims. Despite her calm, which I knew masked a deep fear of dying, she unnerved me. For the first time I was dealing with a patient who I knew could not "get better"—at least not in the traditional sense. I was forced to redefine what I meant by success in therapy. All I could hope to achieve was a peaceful passing for Grace, which might help her choose a more peaceful, untraumatic next life.

Death is the great unresolved trauma. Just as birth is the first major stress experience in our lives, death is the moment when we leave everything unfinished. If death comes suddenly, we take the unresolved situation into another life. Unconsciously we try to solve the past-life problem in the present. If we die in a long, protracted agony, we take with us the feelings of bitterness and resentment that almost always accompany such situations.

One of the reasons death is so agonizing for so many people is that the dying triggers a replay of past deaths. The patient is burdened with the confusion, pain, fear, and uncertainty of many prior death experiences. My ambition with Grace was to clear away as much of her passion about death as I could before she had to face the event in this life. Since reincarnation cannot be proven, it was an act of faith to assume that I might influence a future life. Really it didn't matter to me as much as the fact that she might be more comfortable in this life; Grace was going to die, but she was not dead yet. She was a woman with a hard reality to face, deserving every consideration.

I have already explored one case of uterine cancer in this book, a case where the disease regressed at the completion of therapy. Many of the circumstances surrounding that case were similar to those which Grace described to me. She was a woman with an obsession about her failure with children. She had one daughter but felt enormous guilt that she had been unwilling to have more. In her words:

> I feel now, always felt, like a failure because I only got to "hurt" once, delivering that one child. But I couldn't face it again. That pain, it felt like my insides were being torn out in a long, slow torture process. I felt myself give up control of my body to strangers, let them do what they wanted . . . and I said, "Never again." I said, "I'll live without doing that again!" But I never really felt peaceful about it. I knew other women did it. Some of them did it over and over. I couldn't.

It seemed likely that Grace's agony in childbirth was due, in part, to the replaying of traumatic childbirth experiences in past lives. Before beginning Grace's first session I asked her to describe her own mother to me, hoping to pick up something about the relationship of mother and child.

> I know my mother's first pregnancy was nerve-wracking, because she never tired of telling me about it. The agony of childbirth, sex, and marriage in general—that was her favorite song. She started when I was young . . . I guess she was taking it out on my father . . . trying to turn us against him. By the time I had my first sexual experiences I was pretty well terrified. It felt like I was being kicked by a horse the whole time.

I never forgot that pain, even though I had a good adult sex life. When everything went . . . went down the drain, and I knew I was sick—it felt like a festering sore that wouldn't go away. I could feel it inside me. Even after the operation—I knew it was still there.

We began the session with the sense of festering, and the fear of uterine disorder. As she let her unconscious mind take her where these feelings led her, Grace found herself on her back in a clinic for the poor, undergoing a pelvic examination.

I'm in England, no, maybe Germany . . . it's maybe the seventeenth century . . . at least I see people wearing long robes. . . . I'm on a mat . . . there are many around me on mats . . . a lot of moaning . . . so many people in pain. . . . I feel hands on my shoulders holding me down . . . hands on my legs . . . holding them apart. . . . I feel so ashamed . . . they're looking inside me, men . . . looking inside me. . . . I have a terrible disease and I'm so ashamed . . . the doctor won't even look at me because I'm so poor. There's a man looking down at me, sneering. I hate him. I hate him and I don't even know him. He's the one who's making me so ashamed . . . I think he's a medical assistant of some sort. . . . He's saying, "The doctor was right, he didn't even have to see her . . . she's eaten up with the 'curse' . . . most women like her are. That's all they're good for. All we can do is burn it out and wait for her to die. She's too far gone to save." Another man looks into me. He asks, "Why bother? She's going to die anyway." The first man says, "She might spread it. If we burn it she won't be able to pass it around. . . ." I feel a terrible pain in my vagina . . . like a pole is being thrust up it and moved around inside my uterus . . . I can't stand it. I can't . . . I'm fading away, I guess I faint. I hear voices dimly through a haze. . . . "There should be a way to take the whole thing out. That'd stop her for good." I'm semi-conscious now. . . . I hear voices saying, "Is she still here? She sure is taking her time. She must like suffering or she'd hurry it up." I'm constantly aware of a searing pain in my uterus. A man's voice says: "She's finally started bleeding . . . it won't be long now." The pain is getting worse . . . I'll welcome death when it comes. . . .

We found the patterns of extreme damage to the uterus, the burning sensation in the pelvis, and excruciating pain at childbirth in subsequent sessions.

I'm tied down . . . spread-eagled on the ground . . . there's a great deal of confusion around me. . . . I'm twelve or thirteen years old . . . I hurt . . . I don't know where I am. . . . The pain is at the base of my spine . . . I'm pregnant. . . . It's the baby's weight pressing . . . in my lower-back area. . . . I hear a man's voice saying . . . "She's worthless . . . it's the baby we want. . . . Don't waste time." I see sand and feel a hot wind . . . I'm part of a desert tribe . . . this man is the leader. . . . I'm supposed to bear him a son. I'm so young . . . unprepared—they're forcing me open. . . . He's saying, "We can't save them both. She's too small. She'll never deliver the baby alive."

Suddenly Grace let out a scream. She was so involved in the past-life experience of childbirth that she had forgotten her presence in my office. The shout of pain made her aware of her surroundings. She breathed heavily for a few moments before continuing slowly.

They've cut me open. That's what that was about. The shouting. It's a freezing sensation, and the worst pain, the very worst pain. My belly is all open. A man's saying. "It's the only way." They're reaching inside me, wrenching the baby away. I can see my intestines . . . torn, on the ground.

This incident had informed Grace's reaction to her childbirth experience in the present life, an agony which she vowed never to repeat. At an unconscious level she had always blamed her daughter for this pain. After the session Grace and the girl had a long series of talks; their relationship progressed for the first time in years, with mutual respect replacing resentment and coldness.

The term of Grace's therapy was limited by her health. As her ability to function outside of the home diminished, she worked hard to put her affairs in order. In our sessions we cleared away incident after incident involving damage to the uterus, and the guilt or pain of childbirth. She was beginning to experience a certain amount of pain as the deterioration in her body worsened, but she was determined not to become a regular drug user. As her therapy drew to a close we examined her prenatal history.

> My mother's on the examining table. She's getting a pelvic . . . the doctor is saying, "I don't understand where the redness comes from . . . it just won't go away. . . . It looks like a very stubborn infection." There's something scraping in there . . . something very hot. . . . I hear the doctor saying, "D and C" . . . she's having a D and C . . . they don't know I'm here, don't know she's pregnant. . . . The doctor's saying, "I'm sorry it hurts, but it's necessary if we're going to clean you out." My God, I'm in here and no one knows. And Mother's just thinking—"A good woman shouldn't have anything wrong down there! What could I have done to infect me down there. I'm clean, God knows."

The moment of impact, when Grace's mother was told that she was pregnant, not "infected," was recorded as well.

> I can feel the walls tense. Mother's thinking, "I don't know, maybe they killed it when they burned it. I was sure it was an infection—now it turns out to be pregnancy; I'll never know what was going on inside me. I wonder . . . could they have burned it out?"

Mother's confusion and ambivalence bled into the unconscious mind of the fetus. The association between infection and unborn child—the notion that the fetus itself might be an infection—began to set the pattern of Grace's life. Lives ending with uterine infection or painful and diseased childbirth were restimulated by this mother's confusion during the prenatal.

With her therapy complete, Grace continued to move about for a short time. Soon, however, she was confined to her house, and was induced to take some medication for increasing pain. Whether her pain was actually less acute than that of most cancer sufferers, or whether she simply had less difficulty bearing it, is impossible to say. Pain is a subjective experience. But her physician reported that, through the moment of death, Grace took fewer drugs, in smaller doses, than any patient he had ever tended in such a situation.

Grace felt very little panic as she saw death approaching. It would be unfair to say that she didn't mind dying. Life is dear to each of us, even if we do believe that we will come back. But she had made a peace with her own fate, and knew that *if* the theory of reincarnation was accurate, she would return in a body untroubled by the guilt and pain that she had found going back hundreds of years. The case provided a sidelight for me as well; I came to believe that I had no past unresolved problems regarding cancer. Had there been any I'm sure I would never have been able to remain objective and supportive of Grace through the tension of this death experience.

The experience of dying is, of course, unpredictable. A parent may have some control over his child's conception, prenatal period, and even birth, but death comes about in too many different ways; few are informed of its approach. The unresolved trauma at death is a primary cause of behavioral disorder. Most of the problems I encounter have their source in past-life deaths; when the impact of these deaths is erased, many disorders simply evaporate. I believe that if we could all die as Grace Hart did, we would be a much more rational civilized race. It is, of course, not possible. At the moment of death few are prepared; most are doomed to leave everything unfinished.

16

THE SPACE
BETWEEN LIVES

MEMORIES OF PRENATAL AND BIRTH EXPERIENCES CAN, TO
some extent, be corroborated. It is virtually impossible to
prove anything about the space between lives, however. It
is not measurable, not observable to the living; it is an of-
fensive notion to many with traditional religious beliefs,
and a foolish one to many others.

My experience with this "space" has been far too shallow
to make any definitive statements. Patients describe a life
outside the body as easily as they describe their births and
deaths. I rarely let patients linger in this area, however, although it is very tempting, with its mysteries and its promises
of sudden revelation. In fact, in my experience, life outside
the body reveals very little. It does not seem to be a state
of exalted wisdom or extraordinary perception at all. The
problems that plague a particular life are carried into the
space between lives. Our inability to deal with these problems influences our choice of the next body we enter. I
realize the scope of this claim, and that it is unprovable, but
for an illustration of the mechanics of it, consider the case
of Greg Marston.

Greg came to me because of repeated business failures.
He was a huge man with an aggressive manner and a loud,
commanding voice. The pattern of his business ventures was
repetitive. He insisted upon being a tycoon and used whatever money he could raise not to build a successful operation,
but to create the impression that he controlled a multi-
divisional corporation. At the time of treatment he was in
the process of draining all funds from a small grocery store

that he owned, creating a paper empire. He spent enormous sums publishing his own writings, which no publisher would accept, and was using whatever cash he could turn up to start "divisions" of his corporation: Marston Publishing, Marston Retail Outlets, Marston Paper Products, and several others. These company names were, of course, completely without substance. With the exception of the publishing firm, they were all part of a small grocery store.

When I queried him about his rationale, these phrases emerged: "I'm always under attack. I've got to re-establish myself as top man. People have to know that I'm a leader in the field. This kind of business policy demands respect from little people."

Beginning with the phrase, "I'm always under attack," we brought Greg back to a time when gladiator battles entertained the masses.

I'm in an arena. I don't know what's going on, really, but I'm used to it . . . I guess I'm stupid or something. But I'm big, like I am now. A big hulking guy. They're strapping this armor around me, a bunch of men, much smaller than me. A crowd is cheering. I can hear people talking about me. . . . "He's our best fighter . . . always gives a great show . . . the top man we've got. . . ." They're speaking some other language, but that's it . . . that's what they mean. I'm top man.

They're opening a gate. I'm all alone in this arena, but the crowd's started screaming. Midgets are streaming out from the gate at me. I'm supposed to fight about thirty midgets. They're jumping on me, climbing on me, clawing at me. I'm swinging a club . . . everyone seems to be loving this. . . . There's too many for me. I'm confused—I didn't think this was going to happen. I don't know what I expected. . . . They're stabbing me. Someone, my boss . . . the one who turned me loose . . . he's yelling, "Get back in there, get up and fight. Hurry or it'll be too late. Hurry, hurry. . . ." I can't seem to make contact. I . . . I'm not moving anymore. . . .

DR. NETHERTON: Are you still in your body?

GREG MARSTON: I'm confused . . . I don't know . . .

DR. NETHERTON: Can you see your body?

GREG: It's there. I can see it, lying in the arena. Blood is pouring out of my chest and stomach. He's still shouting at me—"Hurry, hurry" . . . no one knows I'm not there anymore.

DR. NETHERTON: What's it like?

GREG: Like the sound of wind rushing around me. All I'm thinking, though—I'm not paying attention—I'm thinking, "I've got to get back, they're still fighting, I've got to get back there and show them. I'm flying outward . . . it isn't exactly up—it's just out . . . somewhere.

DR. NETHERTON: What are you aware of now?

GREG: I see a battlefield. This is somewhere else. Someone's saying it again, though . . . "Hurry hurry." It's a woman, in a tent. She's making love to a man in a uniform, saying, "Hurry, hurry," and now . . . a jolt! I felt a jolt, like, almost like a sudden electric shock, just for a second. I'm inside her. I'm inside this woman . . . in the womb.

DR. NETHERTON: Tell me the first thing you hear or feel.

GREG: The man's saying, "I've got to get back. I've got to. . . . The battle will start soon. Men depend on me to lead them." He's pulling on his clothes. There's a blast. I hear screaming. Screaming. The battle's started, or something. Mother's dead . . . I'm dead, too, I guess. Explosions, flashes of light . . . I was only there for a second.

Greg had described a very brief out-of-body experience. He had risen "outward" from the battle situation in an ancient arena, wanting badly to continue battle. His sudden freedom from the body did *not*, however, release him from this desire. His concentration was on return to battle, even though it was no longer possible to return to the battle in which he had been killed. Through this concentration he seems to have "chosen" his next life; he was conceived on a battlefield, brought back to an emotional state similar to the one he had left. Unconsciously Greg wanted to continue his unfortunate, embattled situation. His attitude in the space between lives was no different from his attitude while alive. Out of the body he gained no wisdom whatever.

He continued to find himself returning to battles, and he vividly described his death in World War I and the period immediately following.

GREG: Now I hear battle sounds, big guns, rifles, I think it's World War One. I'm on a battlefield, I'm alive, there are many dead men around. . . . The company commander is dead. I'm thinking, "Good, he's dead, I'm top man now, you guys are taking orders from me."

DR. NETHERTON: What do the other men say to this?

GREG: "He finally got a commission. Let the s.o.b. become commander, us little guys will let him win the war singlehanded."

DR. NETHERTON: What's happening now?

GREG: I want to move to higher ground to be on top of things. I'm standing up, feeling boastful, very proud, I want to see if the way is clear. There are two shots . . . I'm hit.

DR NETHERTON: Where do they hit?

GREG: One in the chest, the other in the stomach. I feel great pain. As I'm dying I hear the men around me talking.

DR. NETHERTON: What are they saying?

GREG: "Good-bye, s.o.b. Hurry back and lead us again sometime. . . ."

DR. NETHERTON: Where are you now?

GREG: I'm shooting up into the sky like a bullet! I see my body below, there's the battlefield and the men marching past the body. I'm moving through a dark tunnel, now there's light. I see a line of military men. They're men I've been in battle with. I'm pleading with them.

DR. NETHERTON: What are you saying?

GREG: "Let me go back, please, let me go back, let me go

back." They're telling me to take my time, to make a rational decision, to review my life, to look at what I'm doing.

DR. NETHERTON: What do you answer?

GREG: "I'm going back, you can't make me stay here, you're no better than I am, I'm going back."

DR. NETHERTON: What are they saying now?

GREG: One of them is saying, "Well, let the s.o.b. go back already."

DR. NETHERTON: And now . . . ?

GREG: I hear a woman.

DR. NETHERTON: What's she saying?

GREG: "You son of a bitch, get off me, get back already, you're hurting me . . ." I feel that jolt again. The same shock. This is my own mother. I'm in this life. In the womb.

From cases like Greg's I have been able to draw some ideas about this life between lives, which many think of as "life after death." I feel the expression "life outside the body" is more accurate, since, as far as my patients are concerned, it is not "after death" but, simply, between lives.

The most difficult aspect of this "life" for most people to reconcile themselves to is that it is not particularly different from life in the body. The individual has many of the same concerns, sees life in many of the same terms. Greg's lives in the body were involved with wars and fighting; outside the body he encountered war heroes and fellow soldiers. He was no better at making decisions between lives than he had been on the battlefield. This pattern is consistent. People usually gain no particular wisdom in this void. They tend to "choose" a next life using criteria provided by the trauma of their previous death, unable to rationally consider how unhappy this will make them. For those who wish to avoid responsibility for their own problems, the space between lives can be a most disheartening revelation.

Sometimes the between-lives experience emerges spontaneously in the therapy, as in Greg's case. Sometimes an individual wants to go there out of curiosity, to complete spiritual work, or for a better understanding of life. Usually I discourage this.

A few of the people who come to Past Lives Therapy are "spiritual addicts." They are mesmerized by the occult. I have a great deal of trouble getting these people to confront their problems realistically. They would prefer to go into the out-of-body state and remain there forever. Many refuse to believe that no superior wisdom is to be found in this state, and no ability to influence events. One came to me claiming that her uncle Harry visited her in spirit form, advising her to sell her house. I asked her whether her uncle had had any real estate expertise when alive, and she informed me that he had lost quite a lot of money in that business. Nonetheless, she convinced herself that his "spiritual advice" was beyond question. I did not wish to begin a debate on the "spirit world" and declined to take her on as a patient.

"Occultist" attitudes prevail in discussions of the life outside the body, and no research of respectable quality has been done on reports of this state. The temptation to linger in this mystical area is reason enough for avoiding it in most cases. There are, however, a few people whom I deliberately guide into this area. Usually I make this move when I feel the patient has no desire to linger there, and when there is some problem that will not fully resolve itself with the usual techniques of the therapy.

When I encourage a patient to enter this area, I continually find the same thing. We are no different out of the body than in; unwilling to learn from our in-the-body experience, we repeat our patterns out of the body, until we can find a body to enter that will allow us to repeat in-the-body patterns all over again.

In the previous chapter I discussed a patient who was dying; my attempt in that case was to "clear" her past-life patterns before death, so that she would be entering this "between-lives" state with a fresh outlook. The effects of such an attempt will remain unknown. One of the frustrations of working as a Past Lives therapist is that I can't be certain how far my work reaches. We have found significant improvement in patients who work in Past Lives Therapy, as amply demonstrated in the "Casework" section of this book. I can only hope that these behavioral improvements will be carried over into future lives. I am satisfied that they vastly change the current life of each patient.

IV

INFERENCES, BY-PRODUCTS, IMPLICATIONS

ALTHOUGH THE AIM OF PAST LIVES THERAPY IS SOLELY TO help people deal with the reality of their lives in the here and now, practice of the therapy brings me into contact with many large, and largely unanswerable, questions. However, I have not devoted much of my time to doing organized research on the question of reincarnation. As I have stated previously, the "truth" or "fiction" of reincarnation is virtually irrelevant to the success of Past Lives Therapy. Nonetheless, I must deal with the question every day of my life and, in fact, it is a subject of great appeal. Many events that have taken place in sessions with patients force me to examine and re-examine it.

Have we lived before? This section of *Past Lives Therapy* touches on some of the research currently being done on the subject and concludes with a series of experiences I have had with my patients. I wish to be clear on one point. Nothing I do is done in the name of experiment. Nothing I have done can be classified as organized research. The experiences I have had, and the situations I have been witness to, are by-products of a therapeutic method. I *feel* the validity of past lives in my patients' voices, in their actions as they lie on the couch, and in their conscious reactions to what their unconscious minds reveal. The scientific interpretation of data is the next step, but it must be left for someone else; it is full-time work. I could never devote the amount of time and energy necessary for the job.

REINCARNATION IN WESTERN THOUGHT: A BRIEF SUMMARY

Hard research into reincarnation is in its infancy; the philosophical concept of reincarnation, however, is ancient. It is most commonly associated with the Eastern religions, but is by no means unknown in Western thought. Among the ancient Greeks, Pythagoras led an influential religious cult supporting the doctrine of reincarnation. The Kabala, a collection of Jewish mystical lore, also acknowledges the idea of past lives, and the early Christians debated the notion for several centuries. Many supported the doctrine of the third-century teacher Origen, who attempted to blend the Christian and Greek philosophies into a coherent whole. Reincarnation was an integral part of his teaching. In A.D. 533, however, a council of the church, meeting in Constantinople, pronounced Origen's teachings anathema to Christian belief, and reincarnation went underground in the West. It re-emerged during the Renaissance, and by the eighteenth century it was no longer dangerous, although hardly fashionable, to hold the belief that we live more than once. In

succeeding centuries several mystical religions teaching reincarnation gained moderate popularity in the West, including Theosophy and, most recently, Scientology. In each of
these cults and religions, however, the question of reincarnation has been a philosophical one. It is put forth as an
article of faith, never tested by scientific method. All of the
religious debate, the philosophical observation, and the mus-
ings of poets and scholars have been directed at questions of
"belief" and not of "proof." Proof is not a matter for emotion
or faith to decide.

Can we prove reincarnation? With the data available to
us at this time the answer has to be "no." But unlike concepts of heaven and hell, the identification of past incarnations seems within our grasp. Heaven, by definition, exists in
a plane unreachable to the living. Past lives, on the other
hand, can be pinpointed; they take place on earth, in places
that can be found, explored, and studied. There are problems
facing reincarnation researchers, however. It is impossible to
determine how much a subject may have read, heard from
family and friends, gathered from movies and theater, or
otherwise digested about the scenes that he recounts in such
detail. Without isolating potential subjects from society and
family at birth, which is, of course, unthinkable, there doesn't
seem to be any way to control these factors. Nonetheless,
several psychologists are experimenting with patients who
describe previous incarnations in ancient and recent times,
using historical reference texts to check the validity of their
patients' observations. Their results cannot be classified as
"proof." Still, the idea of reincarnation seems the simplest
explanation for the data.

CURRENT RESEARCH

Most reincarnation research has been done by regressing
subjects via hypnosis. While I do not approve of hypnosis
as a therapeutic method, it is a valid means of reaching the
unconscious mind for experimental purposes. Even without
hypnosis, some researchers have had success, especially with

children, in finding recent past lives. We speak frequently of children's "fantastic imaginations." We rarely listen to our children's stories with any seriousness, and if a child were to tell of a life as a shoemaker, for instance, in a different time or place, we would simply attribute the story to something the child had picked up from television, other children's talk, comic books, or the like.

In his book *Twenty Cases Suggestive of Reincarnation*, Dr. Ian Stevenson reports on his travels to places where reincarnation is still a common belief—Buddhist and Hindu countries such as India, Ceylon, and Lebanon. Dr. Stevenson, a professor in the department of Neurology and Psychiatry at the University of Virginia School of Medicine, felt that the children of these countries would be more "open" than children in the West. Our society tends to cut off or disregard the "unrealistic" aspects of a child's conversation, and our children soon forget.

Stevenson interviewed many children and found their tales, dreams, and memories highly suggestive of reincarnation. His most intriguing case concerns Imad Elwar, a five-year-old Arab boy living in the village of Kornayal, Lebanon, in 1964. Before the boy was two, he'd begun to mention his past lives. His first words referred to his mistress in a prior incarnation. Born December 21, 1958, the boy claimed to be from the village of Khriby, some twenty-five miles away. He claimed to have been Ibrahim Bouhanzy, who had died of tuberculosis on September 8, 1944.

The boy correctly supplied Bouhanzy's dying words, identified the surviving members of his family, and never ceased to refer affectionately to Jarmile, Ibrahim's mistress. Dr. Stevenson traveled with the boy and his family to Ibrahim's village and tabulated fifty-seven items that the boy recalled from memory. Of these, fifty-one checked out as accurate, including details of the interior of Bouhanzy's house. Dr. Stevenson could find no good explanation, other than reincarnation, for this situation or for other similar ones. His book remains the best documented work in the field.

Helen Wambach, a clinical psychologist, offers more support for the possibility of reincarnation. Her technique has been to hypnotize entire groups of people and to ask them for details of lives in four distinct time periods—A.D. 1850, 1700, and 25, and 500 B.C. She feels that most Americans have pre-conceived associations with three of these time periods from popular literature and movies—the early West in 1850, colonial America in 1700, the Holy Land or Rome in A.D. 25. If the great majority of the lives her subjects remembered were set in these places, it would begin to support the thesis that "past lives" are in fact products of the imagination or stories remembered from youth. The results of her experiment showed quite the opposite, however. In the 1850 time period only half of the subjects found themselves in North America at all, and most of those were in the South or the East. Twenty-three percent of the subjects found themselves in Europe, and the others were scattered over the globe. In the 1700 time period only 16 percent of the subjects reported lives in America; several of these were Indians. Almost half were European, and the others again ranged from the Near East to South America. None of the subjects recalled lives in A.D. 25 in which they had even heard of Christ, and in 500 B.C. the subjects reported lives widely scattered, the majority living in the Near East and Asia.

"If people were reporting stories they had read," Wambach wrote, "they weren't the stories most common in our culture. Either all my subjects were quite sophisticated and managed individually, without consultation with each other, to come up with lives scattered neatly in the appropriate historical pattern, or hypnosis does tap real memories of the past."

In my own work, unexplained events continue to take place during sessions. I have learned to take them in stride. I believe it is foolish to deny something simply because I cannot comprehend it. The unknown quantities of our life far outweigh the little we know about ourselves and our world. The extraordinary situations that follow are no more than that—extraordinary situations. They do not "prove" anything in the sense that we can "prove" that wood burns. They simply indicate the magnitude of the questions we must ask ourselves.

MULTIPLE VIEWPOINTS

Among past-life recollections I have witnessed, the most common phenomenon is a multiple viewpoint of the same event from several different patients. I have already illustrated such a case in the chapter "Relationships." Much more mysterious is the case below, in which the patients relating the scene to me did not know each other and were not even in therapy at the same time. Although the event that each patient was describing was the crucifixion of Christ, none of the five seemed to have played an important or historically recorded part in the event. The first recall was given to me by a young man in April of 1970. Without knowing where it would lead, he had begun describing an incident on a hot, dusty dirt road. He was wearing sandals and a gown or robe.

I feel very anxious to get back and join the others. I've been gone somewhere, for days, delivering something, I don't know what, a letter or message, or something. I feel I've done my job well, and "he" will be very proud of me . . . now there's a man running toward me, coming down the road. I recognize him, he's one of the group. He's waving his arms, calling to me. His face is red. "Come quickly, come quickly! They're killing him. We couldn't stop it. Hurry!" Now I'm running toward him. I can't believe it. Something must have happened while I was away. They're killing him!

We're running, running. Up hills, over stones. This isn't the path, it's like a shortcut. Now I can see them on top of the hill. In a clearing. Crosses. Not three, though. About forty. Scattered over the hill and running down one side. I can see Jesus, screaming in agony. There's blood running down his body.

I'm calling as I run, "Dear God, not now, it's too soon, don't let him die. Let me get to him."

I'm pushing my way through the crowd. A lot of people are gathered, curious people. I'm just pushing and shoving past them, making a run at the cross. A guard— I can see him out of the corner of my eye, but he's too quick. He's swinging at me, a spear . . . pain . . . and I'm fallen. I'm out cold. He's knocked me out.

When the patient awakened, he was all alone. The cross was still erected, but it was empty.

I know what's happened, though. I know where the cave is. This is part of the plan. I never thought we'd have to use it . . . it was just a plan we made up. I can't believe it's happened. I'm entering the cave now . . . I see a lot of people I know. Someone, a man, I can't see who, says, "Oh my God, he's dead. What do we do now?" We're wrapping him in white cloth. Wrapping the body. It's part of the plan.

It may seem a grandiose fantasy to have been one of Jesus' followers, and to have been in the cave from which he supposedly rose after three days. The patient's therapy was successful, and I did not attempt to deal with the question of whether he had actually seen Christ on the cross. I had all but forgotten the incident, as a matter of fact, when, three years later, a second patient wandered into the same territory. The story he recounted prompted me to comb my files for notes on the above case. The two patients were from different walks of life, had never heard of each other, and neither was particularly schooled in religious thought or history. Nonetheless, the second patient confronted the following scene.

I'm watching people in agony. I must be a child, maybe twelve or thirteen, and my mother's standing by me, trying to divert my attention, to get me to leave. But I'm glued to this spectacle: men on crosses. Lots of them, nailed to the cross and sagging forward. I'm asking her, "Who are they?"

She says, "I don't know, you shouldn't be seeing this. Come away." But I won't move. She's pulling me, but she's kind of caught up in it too. Now somebody's got his hand in my face, pushing me away . . . he's moving past me, a man, much bigger than I am. He's shouting—"Oh, God, not now, don't kill him now!" and he's knocked me down. He's running toward one of the crosses. One of the guards takes a quick step, slashes him across the head with a spear. My mama shouts, "Now there's going to be a fight, let's go." This is too much . . . I can't tell why anyone would hit him, or why they're hanging. Mama's dragging me away, though. She's right, too—it's very upsetting . . .

This patient had no idea he was watching the crucifixion of Christ. Because of the forty crosses, instead of the three that are supposed to have been there, he never associated the scene with Jesus or Christianity. Nor would I, except for the description of the man being knocked out by the spear.

Eight months later I found myself working with a female patient who expressed a strong desire to run from men. We found her watching a man being hoisted and nailed onto a cross. He was one of many being crucified. The patient reported that she was hiding in the crowd surrounding the crosses. Several men were pursuing her. She did not associate the scene with Jesus and had no feelings that she was involved with the early Christian movement. It could have been any mass execution.

I'm watching, thinking, "How awful, this man's death is my excuse for standing in the crowd. I don't know anything about him—what he's done, who he is—I'm just using him." Now I hear someone say, "Look at that fool." There's a commotion; I'm turning around. It might be the men who are chasing me, but it's not. There's a man pushing his way through one of the crowds in front of another cross. He's yelling something, but I can't hear the words— he's on the other side, by the other crosses. A guard has hit him. He's bleeding from the head, lying on the ground. I think he's dead. I want to go help him, but I'm afraid.

Why do I want to help him? He's just like other men. I'm beginning to slip out of the crowd. I'm running again. Running into the country.

This description, although less detailed, is similar to the first two. For some reason the man struck down by the guard seems to have been a resounding image for a great number of people who recall the crucifixion, much more powerful than the body of Jesus, which they are unaware of.

A full year went by before I again encountered a tie-in to my first patient's description of Christ's death, and this fourth patient, also a woman, described the second, rather than the first half of the story.

I'm in a small, dank cave. There's not much light. I'm trying to see what's going on in the center. A group of people are gathered around. I don't know if I've run away from home . . . I'm nine years old, and I don't know anyone here, or even what's happening. They're too busy to notice me. I'm getting down on my hands and knees, crawling forward between the bodies . . . the smell is awful. They're letting me through, though . . . Oh God, there's a dead body. They're gathered around a dead body. My . . . I feel like my heart stopped. I don't know what to do. I hear one of the men saying, "My God, he's dead. What do we do now?" Now all I want to do is get out. I'm crawling toward the entrance. . . . There's a man, he's come in looking dazed. He has a cut above his eye, a swelling, and a glazed look. His head is slashed. I'm leaving . . . I'm escaping into the woods. I feel like I've been in a dead place. A place where death would get me.

The quote, "He's dead—What do we do now?" is, of course, not recorded in the Bible, but it seems to be the only line of dialogue from the cave that may actually have been said. I saw this patient five years after seeing the man who was struck in the head. No logical explanation presented itself to me except that these events had actually happened as my patients were replaying them. This feeling was reinforced in another situation. I was asked to see a patient from a state mental hospital. He was suffering from acute religious fanaticism and a tendency to mutilate himself. I knew nothing about this man, and could barely communicate with him. But during four and a half hours of torturously slow work, the following scene, set at a slightly different time than the others, emerged.

> Lying in a heap of men. Like we've been thrown here . . . in a pile. But I'm not dead. No, sir. I can't move is the only thing. I can't move, and I hurt—my hands are mangled From the nails. They've thrown us down from the crosses. In a pile. None of us can move. I guess most of these bodies are dead ones. Not mine. There are two men looking down at us. The first one says, "Which one's the Jew?" And the second answers, "He's gone. Earlier. They took him away." The first one says, "Well, that's one less for us to have to finish. You'd think they'd die quickly with all that pain and bleeding." The second one laughs. "We always wind up running a sword through them to make sure they're gone. Did you kill the one you hit with the spear?" The first one says, "No, I just put him out. I think he's already gone." The second one says, "Well, he's a damn fool. I wonder what he thought he was doing? Some kind of fanatic, I guess."
>
> Now they're turning us over, one by one. I think everyone's dead. I can feel a hand on my shoulder. I can't see. I sense a black shape over me. Now a plunging, into the chest. I can feel whatever it is go right through me—into the earth underneath. Now I'm gone. I'm not there anymore.

This brought to five the number of people who had made reference to this incident. The incident had little to do with Christ himself. It cannot be accurately called a coincidental series of self-aggrandizing fantasies; three of the five did not even know that it was the crucifixion of Jesus they were witnessing, a fourth made only passing reference to "the Jew." Only the fifth actually had some involvement with Christ, and he is the one whom everyone seems to have noticed. Although this case is unprecedented (in my experience) for its detailed recollection, it is only one of several historical incidents that I have heard from more than one viewpoint with inexplicable agreement about what transpired.

AN INFANT DEATH IN NAG'S HEAD

When cases are presented to me containing facts that *can* be checked, I do attempt to validate the material, even though research is not my primary interest. I don't suggest that my patients remember details and statistics, but the patient sometimes inadvertently volunteers dates, places, or other information that can be documented.

In one case, a female patient described a past-life infancy in a resort community by the ocean. She was aware of feelings that her mother, who was not married, was "sort of insane, lonely, very isolated." The patient remembered being carried along the beach past a large white house almost every day. She overheard the following conversation between her mother and a woman on the beach:

MOTHER: Are you staying at Jarrett House?
WOMAN: Yes. It's so beautiful here.
MOTHER: It's a nice beach.
WOMAN: We're thinking of moving to North Carolina to retire, but we're not sure where.
MOTHER: Well, there's not much to do here in Nag's Head.
WOMAN: I guess not, but at least there's Jarrett House and all that good food.

Several similar conversations were reported, although none as specific as to the location of the resort as this one. The patient, who remained in her mother's arms throughout these conversations, could not decide if her mother worked at Jarrett House or was part of the family that owned it, but she recalled seeing it quite clearly, a large, white ante bellum house whose back porch led directly onto the beach. She distinctly remembered a wraparound front porch with rockers spaced every few feet, and wide double front doors of heavy wood. At this time she reported her age as "about two months." At three months of age she was left outside by her mother and developed a bronchial infection from which she died.

In going over the session the patient claimed that in this life she had never heard of Nag's Head, North Carolina, and certainly not of Jarrett House.

A call to the Chamber of Commerce of Nag's Head revealed that this resort had indeed existed and had stood for almost a century on the beach outside of town. A large white resort mansion, with a wide front porch, it had been renowned primarily for its food. As far as we could tell, no celebrities had vacationed there, making it unlikely that the patient would have read about it or seen it on film or television. It was one of hundreds of comfortable resorts dotting the Eastern seaboard from Virginia to Florida. Yet my patient was able to describe it in detail, remember its name, and even recall a snippet of conversation relating to its cuisine.

A DEPRESSION-ERA SUICIDE IN MIDTOWN

Rarely do I have a patient describe a life from birth through death. More usually I get highlights of trauma, glimpsed in moments of acute pain and unhappiness. But a female patient born in 1936 had evidently lived a life so filled with trial and dread that she was able to document it literally from her birth. She was, she said, the illegitimate daughter of a reasonably well-known actress in New York. She was unable to remember the woman's name, quite possibly because she never saw her. At birth, in 1903, she was given to an older married couple who unofficially adopted her. She lived in rural Pennsylvania until 1916, when her foster parents were killed in an automobile accident, once again thrusting her out and away from a family situation. We picked up the life again in the early Twenties. She'd married a man named McCullum, and moved back to New York City, the place of her birth. She had purchased a small clothing design and manufacturing company in the garment district, off Seventh Avenue in midtown Manhattan. Hard work and a rigid budget saw the couple through until the late Twenties, when the company began to flourish. Then, as it always had, disaster struck.

It's 1928, in the winter. I don't know how I got here . . . but he's dead—Keith is dead. Two doctors are talking to me in a hospital. It happened so suddenly. The cold, the work. He got sick . . . just like a cold. Then he got sicker. I hear "pneumonia," that's the word. They're saying it quite a few times. Nothing could be done. Pneumonia. He worked so hard. No one even knows how to work that hard now . . . we both did.

From this point her life deteriorated at an unbearable rate. In early 1929 her son contracted polio and died. In October of the same year the stock market crashed, and the long economic depression began. Holding together the clothing company was an impossible task, but she did not know what else to do. For over three years she hung on, but by mid-1933 she found herself alone, facing bankruptcy.

I'm in the cutting room. I picked it because of the bars. There are strong bars we've hung the garments from for years. I believe they'll hold me. The date is clear in my mind. June 11, 1933. It's a sunny day. There are a few of those big, black fans in the ceiling. We've turned them off, or the electric company has. It doesn't matter to me. I've got a rope . . .

According to my patient, Rita McCullum hung herself in the cutting room of her factory somewhere off Seventh Avenue in midtown, on June 11, 1933.

Because the pertinent data was available, we contacted the Hall of Records in New York City. Giving them what data we had, we asked if they could verify such a death. We received in the mail a photostated, notarized death certificate for a woman named Rita McCullum, declaring that she had died by hanging at an address in the West Thirties, the heart of the garment district to this day. The date of death was indeed June 11, 1933, and the age was given as thirty, making the birth date sometime in 1903, as the patient had reported. There has been no attempt to verify anything about this particular woman except her death, but the agreement of that detail alone with the story patient narrated seems quite remarkable to me. In my introduction to this book I suggested that there were cases where reincarnation seemed like a *more logical* explanation for a given set of facts than any other. I believe the case of "Rita McCullum" makes this point quite clearly.

THE SINKING OF H.M.S. *REPUBLIC*

A patient who was born and raised in rural Tennessee and now lives in Los Angeles described sailing on a ship from Southampton, England. He had never traveled so grandly before. When I asked him why he was having this new experience, he explained that he was a male nurse traveling with a writer in a wheelchair. Because of his fascination with the luxury ocean liner, he asked many questions of the crew, and was informed, among other things, that the ship had been built in Wales, and that it was one of the first ships to feature both sails and an engine. This placed the time in the early 1800s. (Fulton's first commercial steamboat made its maiden voyage in 1807.) The ship was named the H.M.S. *Republic,* and it sailed under the British flag.

As the ship neared the American mainland, high winds came up, and the storm that followed was tumultuous.

I can sense the panic in the control room, even though I'm not there. I'm in a stateroom, but the pitching is awful, and I'm clinging to the bed, trying to keep the patient in bed without losing control of myself. Now I hear it. A horrible ripping noise like a screeching animal—metal tearing on rock. At once I know we're going down. I don't know what to do—to protect the man in bed or run for it. And in the same instant I know it doesn't make any difference. I'm never getting off this ship.

The patient then described a mad dash through the white corridors of the ship's belly, the shouts of the other passengers as alarms sounded all around him, and finally, the rushing water.

I think we're below water now, but it hasn't reached me yet. I'm hearing it, though. Above, all around. . . . A terrible lurch—I'm thrown over, and we're going down as the water rushes in. I thought we were on the bottom, but now we're going down farther. . . . I must have broken something. I can't move at all. The water's over me. The silence . . . there's a moment of silence underwater. Now I'm dead. We're still sinking. Farther and farther. I sense that some people got off. I don't know how.

A search through records of maritime disasters showed that the H.M.S. *Republic* sank off Cape Hatteras in high seas on February 9, 1813, on a voyage from Southampton, England. Miraculously, 112 people survived this wreck; 238 were lost. The *Republic* did, indeed, feature a combination of sail and steam, and was built in Wales. The patient seemed convinced that the ship had sunk twice, or in two different stages. I wondered why he would seize on this unlikely idea and, at first, I fruitlessly pondered its psychological significance. As it turned out, there was a perfectly natural explanation. According to a description of the sinking, the ship ran against a rock ledge, and sank onto the ledge. But the strong currents pushed it off the underwater shelf, back into the open sea, where it proceeded to plummet some thirty fathoms deeper before coming to rest on the bottom of the ocean off North Carolina.

In this life the patient had not been involved with the sea. The shipping disaster fit into a pattern of behavioral disorder for him (he constantly found himself in "hopeless" situations) but was dissimilar in its setting and details from other lives he described.

THE "PALACE," ABILENE, TEXAS, 1900

Abilene, Texas, was a small town in the year 1900. Despite its size, it boasted a theater called the Palace, which a patient of mine claimed he had owned. According to his memories, the theater business was slack as the turn of the century approached and, in 1900, he was forced to turn the theater over to creditors. As he further described his life, I began to doubt that the decline of show business was responsible for the theater's demise; the patient, who said his name had been James Turner, was a gambler, living a ruinously high life. After losing the Palace, gambling became his profession.

I've strung a man along. He owes me a lot of money. He's a gambler, too. We've played fair—cards, mostly—and I'm in the money pretty good when he pays me. I'd like to get the theater back, but some time's gone by. He hasn't paid me, and now I know. He'll never pay me. It can get cold in Texas, even around Abilene. . . . I never knew it, but I'm sitting in a . . . it's a kind of a saloon. A gray day out, and I'm bundled up in . . . like a coat made of cowhide. It's leather, but trimmed with fur. Everybody knows me here. I'm waiting for him. He comes in the door. It's not a swinging door, like in the movies. . . . This place has a glass door—I can see him, rippled, through the glass. I start to stand up. He's through the door. . . . There's no time. He's got a gun instead of money. I'm confused. I can see the smoke coming out of the barrel. . . . I'm not sure I heard the noise. On the floor. I'm on the floor. I've taken the chair with me. I can feel my muscles move, but . . . I'm not there anymore. I know the date, too. March ninth, nineteen hundred six. I died. He never paid me. I knew it. I knew it.

The death of James Turner, former theater owner, was not possible to pinpoint. The Abilene Chamber of Commerce confirmed that the Palace had been the premier attraction of the town in 1900. The theater remained as a monument long after it had fallen into disuse and it had not been torn down until the 1920s, when a spate of new construction destroyed much of picturesque, "wild West" Abilene. No information could be obtained about the theater's owner, except that it was rumored that he had been killed in a gun battle over a gambling debt. His name was unavailable.

Beginning from the other end, we asked the Hall of Records to trace the name of James Turner, hoping to be rewarded with a death certificate. Unfortunately, there was no systematic recording of deaths in Taylor County at that time. By a stroke of luck, however, we discovered that the same building spree that had destroyed the Palace in the 1920s had also required an entire graveyard in Abilene to be moved. The state was required to record the names of all those transported. Buried in that Abilene cemetery was a man named James Turner, born 1866, died 1906. As of this writing it has not been possible to connect him with the Palace Theater or to find an exact date and cause of death. Should this information be secured, and should it prove the patient's recollection of the circumstances accurate, it would be an extremely suggestive case; it is highly unlikely that a patient would have simply stumbled on facts that continue to elude researchers working with the historical societies of the area.

REMEMBERING THE PRENATAL AND BIRTH

I have a volume of information about the prenatal period and birth of my patients. Many parents are willing to discuss their children's memories of these events. The possibility that a child may have been previously told about these events is ever-present, but, in the cases presented below, the chances are reduced.

I. A CHILD BORN TWICE

I worked with a teen-age girl who had given me a fairly
elaborate account of her prenatal history and then had moved
into a delivery scene that was totally confusing. She described
herself as a male baby. For a moment I thought she was
reliving a past-life birth, but a look at her medical history
revealed that she had correctly identified by name the attending doctors and the hospital where she had been born into
this life. Nonetheless, she insisted that she was a baby boy.
As she emerged from the birth canal, she heard the doctor
say, "The esophagus isn't fully developed. We may lose this
one." She felt great pain and constriction around the throat
and was unable to breathe easily. She then recalled developing a fever, while still in the hospital, and dying there three
days later. Despite the fact that this was obviously not the
birth into her present life, she continued to associate it with
a prenatal period in the womb of this mother. All of her
prenatal memory seemed accurate. We worked on this birth
scene until all attachment to the trauma was gone, but
neither one of us could understand when the scene could
have taken place.

As luck would have it, this patient was too young to drive;
her mother brought her to every session. At the conclusion of
this particular appointment I called the mother in to see if
she might be able to shed some light on this mysterious
situation. I postulated that the mother might have witnessed
such a delivery in an emergency circumstance, or might have
been profoundly affected while she was pregnant by a book
or movie in which such a scene had taken place. These ideas
seemed unlikely, but I didn't know what else to think. I
described the situation in terms of its key oddities—a male
child, a damaged esophagus, a high fever, and death after
three days. The patient's mother burst into tears. After a
few moments she regained her composure and related the
following facts. She had lost a male child in those exact circumstances immediately prior to conceiving the daughter
who was my patient. The boy had been born with a damaged

breathing apparatus and had died as my patient had described. The mother admitted that, after the death, she prayed for her son to come back continually and was in an inconsolable state for several weeks. Because she became convinced that she was in danger of remaining in this depression for the rest of her life, she decided to conceive again, hoping that the responsibility of a new child would force her to "come out of her shell." Throughout the pregnancy she was, quite naturally, obsessed with the fear that history might repeat itself. She thought continually of the passage of the first pregnancy and replayed the delivery scene over and over in her head. Determined that the child would not be burdened with the grief that she, herself, was suffering, she had vowed never to tell her of the first child's brief, unhappy life.

Once detached from this scene, the patient was able to play out the prenatal period and the delivery scene pertaining to this life; the delivery took place at the same hospital, and with the same doctor.

Even if it is possible that the mother had told her daughter about the first, injured baby, or that the daughter had heard her discussing it with others, it seems unlikely that she would have heard enough to be able to construct an entire prenatal period and all of the details of the birth with such accuracy. She was able to recall conversations during the first pregnancy as well as the second, and those that we checked were accurate.

II. BIRTH IN A FOREIGN HOSPITAL

A male patient recalled a panicky birth scene in which his mother was heavily drugged. He heard a male voice with an unidentifiable foreign accent saying, "Push, Mrs. Welles, now push, Mrs. Welles. Harder, Mrs. Welles." The words seemed to be those of a doctor coaxing a woman in labor, but the patient's mother was not named Welles, and he could not imagine who "Mrs. Welles" might have been. He felt great confusion as he made his way down the birth canal, and concern for his mother, who seemed to be "absent" (due to the effect of drugs) and who was not even being correctly identified.

All of this played interestingly into the patient's case. He had come to me complaining of various symptoms, and suggested, from time to time, that all of his troubles might disappear if he changed his name. He would "be a different person." I pointed out that his name was not the same thing as his identity, but, although he understood this intellectually, he was unable to rid himself of the feeling that a name change might be a solution to all of his problems.

After a session like the one described above, a "skeptical" therapist might conclude that the patient was expressing, symbolically, the desire to be someone else's child and, consequently, someone else—with a different name. I was convinced that just the opposite was true; that he had really *been* confused about his identity at birth, and from that time forward.

At my request he brought his mother to see me. I asked her to describe the patient's birth, and she confirmed my thesis. The patient was born in Japan when his father was stationed there in the Air Force. The father was not home when the mother went into labor. She was admitted to the hospital with a great deal of difficulty because she spoke no Japanese, and the hospital staff had very little English. The maternity ward was completely full, so she was placed in the surgery ward. It was late at night. and the doctor in charge of the ward, who was Japanese, had been drinking. The mother began to panic. She could see that conditions in the hospital were less than adequate, and that she was powerless to do anything about it. She surrendered herself to the situation, but was so nervous that she was drugged immediately. In the delivery room, the doctor picked up her chart and mistakenly read the first name he saw, which was Welles. He presumed that the name of his patient was Welles, and continued to refer to her by that name throughout the delivery. Two American nurses, assisting the doctor, were aware of the error, because "Mrs. Welles" was not a patient at all. She was the nurse who had made the last entry on the chart. The nurses evidently felt that correcting the doctor would further confuse matters, and they remained silent throughout the delivery.

When the delivery was safely completed, the doctor left the room. The mother recalled hearing one nurse say to the other, "Wait until Welles finds out she just gave birth to a new baby. That poor man changed everybody's name, didn't he? He's only had Welles doing his scrub work for about a month now, you'd think he'd know her."

The mother did not remember telling this story to her son, and was puzzled that he had recalled it. She had not thought to make the association between his desire for a name change and this crucial birth incident. The patient and I had often discussed his desire to change his name prior to this session, and he had never brought up the incident of his birth. I can only conclude that he had never heard about it. Once we worked the birth scene, he expressed no further discontent with his name.

III. INFANT HEART MURMUR

As he recalled traveling through the birth canal, a male patient described a "fluttering" in his chest which upset him and alerted him to the fact that something "different, scary" was happening to him. He felt dizzy, and could barely hear a doctor and nurses, who were unaware of his condition, coaxing his mother in her efforts to give birth.

As he emerged at birth he heard the doctor saying, "His heart is racing. He has a fast murmur. Got to do something to slow it down." The patient was aware of being passed from hand to hand for a few moments, and then being placed in a blanket which was wrapped around him and held at both ends so that he swung freely. He described being swung around rapidly in a circle. He could not tell if two people were holding the blanket or only one, but he heard soothing words, or sounds, as he flipped back and forth in the blanket. He at first expressed a sense of panic at this treatment, but the "excitement in the chest" subsided almost immediately, and his heartbeat returned to normal. In another few moments the doctor took him from the blanket and held him. The patient recalled the doctor saying, "Now it's normal. There."

Neither the patient nor I had ever heard of this method of regulating infant heartbeat. (I have heard of a similar method of treating hyperactive children by whirling them in a chair to normalize their metabolism.) The doctor, although long retired, was still living in a small town in northern California. He was ninety-one years old. He not only remembered using this method of treatment for newborns with accelerated heartbeat, he specifically remembered the incident of my patient's birth, because the circumstances required special attention. The doctor had previously delivered a stillborn child to the same mother, and she was emotionally unstable about the delivery of my patient. She spent considerable time with the doctor prior to the delivery and, when the child was born with an accelerated heartbeat, a scene of near-panic ensued. When the child's heartbeat returned to normal, the doctor spent a long period reassuring the mother that the baby was healthy, and describing all of its bodily functions in detail until the mother was reassured. The doctor remembered this in great detail, but was quite surprised that the birth scene had stayed with the patient so many years later. He could not clearly explain the workings of the treatment he had given the newborn, but only knew that it was "traditional" for the accelerated heartbeat, and that it worked regularly for him throughout the years of his practice.

IV. THE WAKING DREAM OF AN ADOPTED CHILD

The closest thing we have to a "foolproof" indication of prenatal memory is a case concerning a colleague of mine and his adopted daughter who was four. This "case" came up purely by chance, as I was working formally with neither the man nor his child.

While I was dining at their house, the daughter began to talk in her sleep, using a syntax and style of delivery that might be used by an adult. Uncertain as to whether she was asleep or awake, we entered her room and found her lying with her eyes closed and a troubled look on her face. She was saying, "Let me alone, go away. I don't want to talk about this. I won't say a word about it. Leave me alone." She repeated these phrases, with variations, for half a minute or so. With the father's permission, I began to question the girl.

"Where are you? Are you still in Mommy's tummy?" I asked.

"Yes," she said clearly.

"Who's talking?"

"Mommy is. She's talking to *her* mommy."

"What words are they saying?" I asked.

" 'Let me alone' . . . they're talking . . . they're using the word 'sex.' She's saying 'sex.' "

"What else?"

" 'Let me alone. I don't want to talk about it anymore. Leave me alone.' "

With this the little girl woke up and looked around the room. She said she was having a dream but couldn't remember it clearly. Her mother held her for a few minutes; then she was given some juice and fell back into a peaceful sleep.

I learned that this child had been given up for adoption at birth. Because the parents adopting were concerned with the child's prenatal and birth history, they had had extensive meetings with the woman who had counseled the little girl's biological mother during her pregnancy. The counselor reported that there had been heavy pressure on the mother to give up the child, especially on the part of her parents. They nagged her repeatedly, telling her that an unmarried mother could not possibly bring up a child successfully, that it was a criminal thing to get pregnant before marriage and a terrible cross for the baby to bear. According to the adoption counselor, the mother-to-be reported several violent arguments with her mother toward the end of pregnancy. These culminated with the girl telling her mother that she would "pretend you're not there until you stop talking about this." On a separate occasion she had complained to the adoption counselor that "they never let me alone. From now on I'm just going to ignore them. They can't argue if I don't answer."

The little girl's waking dream seemed to be a playback of these prenatal events. Because the child was adopted shortly after birth, it is impossible that she heard talk of these fights from her mother or grandparents—she had never seen them. Quite possibly, then, this girl could shed further light on prenatal memory—but I would be unwilling to work with her unless there was a behavioral problem she wanted to correct.

I see the material from my own files primarily as a starting point for further investigation. I hope I have raised some legitimate issues that may be dealt with by scientists, philosophers, medical men, and others whose minds are open. The events seem extraordinary to me. What they mean I do not know. For the therapist, the reliving of past lives is merely a technique, designed to help patients regain lost perspective. The implications of the incidents relived may be much greater; I remain content, however, to work with individual patients on individual problems.

QUESTIONS

In the lectures I have given on Past Lives Therapy in recent years, I have devoted a large portion of the time to fielding questions from the audience. Because Past Lives Therapy is a complex process, many of the questions I receive relate specifically to the technique itself. I have covered most of these in the pages of this book. Many other questions are asked, however, concerning the validity of the therapy, the "feelings" associated with the therapy, and the results of therapy. I have here assembled the most common of these questions and tried to answer each individually.

1. DO YOU HAVE PATIENTS WHO CAN'T RECALL ANY PAST LIVES?

Yes, although few are unable to get beyond this point. Usually, when a patient says he sees or hears "nothing," he has been restimulated to an incident in which he is blind, blindfolded, deaf, or otherwise unable to perceive in the normal ways. In such situations I will ask, "What's happening to your eyes, or ears?" Frequently this will break the barrier: The patient will remember being blindfolded or blinded, and then proceed to remember the other details of the incident.

I do have some patients who cannot ever succeed in recalling any past life. I am convinced, however, that this is a function of shut-off commands recorded in the unconscious, rather than the result of a natural inability. Most frequently, when a patient who has had great difficulty finally *does* reach an incident, the phrases he picks up concern the secretive nature of the incident—"We shouldn't be doing this," "Whatever you do, never tell a soul about this," or, occasionally, "Don't tell a doctor anything, they really don't know what they're talking about." In the case of one patient whose therapy was never really begun because she could not reach past incidents, I discovered that during her prenatal period her mother had converted to a religious philosophy that denied all pain and any feelings that might tempt one away from God. This prenatal experience was, I'm sure, responsible for the total shutdown of access to the unconscious.

2. WHAT DOES THE "SHIFT" INTO THE UNCONSCIOUS ACTUALLY FEEL LIKE TO THE PATIENT GOING THROUGH IT?

Each patient feels it differently. For some it is not very different from a totally conscious state. There is very little slowing of speech or change in syntax patterns. For others it is more clearly differentiated; the voice drops to a lower register, and the words come out in a measured, slightly dreamlike fashion. Some patients start by feeling that they are "making up" parts of what they tell me, but they soon discover that they cannot change the content of their past-life incidents, and must reveal the most personal and painful aspects of the stories they had thought were imaginary. This is what most quickly convinces the skeptic. He begins by saying the first thing that comes into his head simply to placate me. But the moment he comes face to face with his pain, he can no longer deny the validity of the therapy.

Reaching the unconscious mind without hypnotism is quite simple. I do not·do any relaxing exercises with my patients, nor do I use sensory awareness techniques to make the body, or eyelids, feel heavy. There is nothing trancelike, in fact, about a Past Lives Therapy session. At the beginning the patient may have some trouble getting the unconscious memories to flow, but this difficulty is usually eliminated as the patient sees the therapy beginning to work. Once a sense of trust is established between the patient and his own unconscious mind, reaching back to the past becomes a very simple matter.

3. DO YOU WORK WITH TRAUMATIC INCIDENTS IN THIS LIFE?

All the time. Invariably the trauma that a patient describes in this life will have a past-life and prenatal component. Even if the trauma is a totally new one for the patient, it will "remind" his unconscious mind of the most similar incidents in the past. Trauma must be erased in the past, in the prenatal period, *and in the present life,* where it frequently recurs in infancy, childhood, and adulthood.

4. IN COVERING THE PRENATAL PERIOD, ISN'T IT POSSIBLE THAT THE FACTS A PATIENT UNCOVERS ABOUT HIS PARENTS MAY RUIN A PEACEFUL RELATIONSHIP?

Unconsciously, the patient already knows everything about his parents prior to therapy. This knowledge often causes deep problems because it is buried, and only expresses itself in the patient's behavior toward his parents. Misunderstood resentments, hostility that seems to have no source—these are the external signs of an unconscious anger at the parents' past behavior. When the facts are made clear, the patient almost always sees the reason and logic of his parents' actions in perspective for the first time. If a patient comes to me describing a genuinely friendly and secure relationship with his parents, I know that there will be nothing "dredged up" in the course of the therapy to damage that bond. If anything were lurking in the prenatal, the patient would already sense it, and already have an adversary relationship, although he might not understand why.

Normally, people who enter Past Lives Therapy have many problems with their parents. Although we may come across prenatal scenes of aggressive, hostile behavior, often directed at the unborn child, patients emerge from such scenes with great understanding of their parents. They perceive the mother's or father's point of view for the first time. Rarely does a patient respond with anger to recollection of the prenatal period. Many patients find the relationship with parents improving even though that was not the purpose of their therapy. Recall of experience in the prenatal period opens up their perspective. It frequently allows people to feel compassion for their parents for the first time in their lives.

5. HOW MANY PEOPLE EXPERIENCE PAST LIVES AS MEMBERS OF THE OPPOSITE SEX?

I have kept no statistics on this question, but most of my patients recall at least one life as a member of the opposite sex. Helen Wambach reports that 80 percent of her subjects of both sexes reported at least one past life as a member of the opposite sex.

6. WHAT IS THE LIKELIHOOD OF MY ACTUALLY KNOWING SOMEONE FROM A PAST LIFE?

Coincidence simply cannot explain the number of people who seem to know people from previous incarnations. Wambach notes that 85 percent of her subjects report knowing someone from a past life in this life. She does not attempt to corroborate this figure. Some people suggest that the space between lives provides a mechanism for bringing people back together. My own experience supports this in two cases described in this book: the Carl and Abigail Gordon therapy reported in the chapter "Relationships," and the case of the child born twice to the same mother in Part IV, "Inferences, By-products, Implications." Despite cases like these, it is essential to stress that, in therapy, it is the pattern, and not the actual identity of a person that is important. We want to know what the position of "father" or "husband" has meant to you, not if the current male holding that position is identical to one from the past.

7. HAVE PEOPLE DESCRIBED ANIMAL LIVES?

Yes. When I ask someone for the earliest source of input for a particular problem, he almost always describes an animal wound or death. We detach a patient from an animal incident using the same method of repetition employed for human traumatic input.

The fact that animal lives are described to me as the *earliest* level of existence my patients go through brings up an interesting point about the progression of lives. The implication of my patients' experiences is that we all move from the animal level to the tribal level and thence to life in progressively more sophisticated societies. I have never recorded a case of a patient who went from a human life back to an animal life. Lives are rarely described in chronological order; rather they tend to be grouped by traumatic similarities. If we put the lives in order, however, we always find the animal life *before* the first human life.

8. ISN'T THIS "PROGRESSION" YOU DESCRIBE IN DIRECT CONTRADICTION TO THE CONCEPT OF KARMA?

It is. Karma, as understood by the Hindu, Buddhist, and Jainist religions, involves a system of divine judgment. Each man is judged on the basis of all of the acts of his life, and his next bodily state is either his punishment or reward. According to these beliefs, an evil man may be reincarnated as a vicious animal, and a devoted priest may be rewarded with a "perfect" next life. These are the religious beliefs of almost a billion people, and I am not prepared to comment on them one way or another. I can only report my own experience in listening to many hundreds of reports of past lives over the years. From these, I have evolved my own belief of what "karma" means.

Karma is a debt owed to the self, to be paid off by the self at a time when the self decides, and in a manner that the self chooses. It can never be used as an excuse, because everyone has the ability to pay the debt, to come to peace with himself whenever he decides to do so. As long as the debt remains unpaid, it is only he who is not paying it. To pay the debt one must resolve the patterns of one's lives, and take responsibility for being the person one is.

9. WHAT DO YOU MEAN BY "TAKING RESPONSIBILITY FOR YOUR OWN LIFE"?

Responsibility is not guilt, blame, shame, or punishment. It is simply knowing that you are the cause of your life. It is you who chose it, not your parents or your maker. You have, in some sense, been the same person for centuries. You must know who that person is, and you must agree with yourself that you will act in a responsible manner, understanding exactly what your strengths and weaknesses are, to reach the personal potential within you.

10. DO YOUR PATIENTS EVER NOTE IMPROVEMENT IN AREAS OF THEIR LIVES THEY ARE NOT SPECIFICALLY WORKING ON?

Patients often receive residual benefits from Past Lives Therapy. Because a traumatic incident that causes death frequently destroys several parts of the body, detachment from that incident may well result in many types of bodily improvement. A patient with acute migraine headaches discovered many deaths by torture, including, but not exclusively involving, damage to the head. As he became detached from these incidents he began to notice improvement in an arthritic condition which he believed was purely a physiological disease. Needless to say, the torture scenes he relived included pain to the joints, stretching of the fingers, and other input that would lead to arthritis in a later life. The patient had had no hope of easing his arthritic pain, and was amazed that this disease could be eased by therapy. This is not an uncommon occurrence. I have witnessed new growth of thinning hair, improved eyesight, and even increased breast size in a woman working out a sexual identity problem. These physical manifestations of mental-health improvement were unasked-for in every case.

11. HOW ARE RELATIONSHIPS WITH OTHERS AFFECTED BY PAST LIVES THERAPY?

Patients frequently feel that the world is changing all around them. Many claim that their therapy has changed their companions, their friends, and their co-workers all for the better. This is, of course, a subjective reaction to their own improvement. What has usually happened is that the patient no longer triggers negative behavior in others. By changing unattractive patterns of hostility or submissiveness, the patient triggers a fresh reaction from people who were used to avoiding or undermining him. Impressed with the improvement of a patient's attitude, his mate may suddenly become more cooperative, his superiors may find him more worthy of promotion. The improvements brought about by any kind of successful therapy can be measured in the same way. But because the improvement in Past Lives Therapy is so rapid, reactions by others can seem quite dramatic.

12. THERE HAS BEEN A GREAT RESURGENCE
OF INTEREST IN CULTURAL HERITAGE.
MANY PEOPLE HAVE BEGUN EXPLORING
THEIR ANCESTRY IN TERMS OF BLOOD-
LINES. DOES THE CONCEPT OF "CHOOS-
ING" A NEW LIFE FROM THE SPACE
BETWEEN LIVES ELIMINATE THE
VALIDITY OF SUCH CONCEPTS AS FAMILY
HERITAGE?

Not entirely. The *physical* characteristics of a newborn child are determined by the genes of his or her parents; this inheritance is the basis of the "bloodline." I would argue that the unconscious mind is not bound by the rules of genetics, however. Many experimental researchers of reincarnation attribute the phenomenon of past-life recall to "genetic memory," claiming that the events people recall from the past are passed on to them by their parents along with the color of their hair and the strength of their teeth. If this were the case, patients would be recalling the lives of their ancestors. My patients' experiences do not support this theory in any way. Their recall tends to cover the spectrum of human existence; white patients remember being black, chicano patients recall being British soldiers in World War II, and so forth. In addition, many patients recall past lives that took place during their parents' lifetimes, material that could not possibly be stored in the parents' genetic code.

On the basis of my work I am forced to conclude that our family, cultural, or blood heritage gives us less information about ourselves than we might wish. Each of us has a second heritage stored in the unconscious mind, one that may or may not be similar to our physical family line. Recall that each of us tries to come back in an environment that will allow us to continue the patterns of the life we have just left. In some cases the most efficient way to accomplish this end might be to return to a similar cultural background. Thus, a Russian Jew, playing out patterns of religious persecution at the time of the Czar, may find it desirable to return as a Russian Jew.

In such a case his cultural heritage and his "past-life" heritage would be virtually identical. However, it would be as likely that he might be born a black man in South Africa, fated to play out the same patterns of oppression, but with a different cast of characters and a different cultural backdrop.

CONCLUSION

AN OLD AND VALUED FRIEND ONCE TOLD ME THE FOLLOWING:
If a seed rests in your hand, and you want its identity known,
you have two choices. You can dissect it in a lab: you will
certainly get some results, but you will also destroy the seed.
Or, you can plant the seed and watch it grow. The latter will
always take longer, but it will tell you more about the nature
of the seed. My hope for this book is only to plant the seed,
so that others can watch the results. Physicians and other
therapists are invited to put this work to the test. I hope they
will not refuse to consider it on the grounds that it deals
with reincarnation.

Some will have strong feelings of cynicism and mistrust for
a different reason. They will realize that, in Past Lives Therapy, they must give up the role of healer. They will be unable
to take credit for the changes brought about in their patients.
Perhaps they will also see that, in the long run, it is always

the patient who cures himself. This work makes available a technique which places all responsibility where it belongs— on the patient. We must never tell the patient that we can do something that he cannot do. Past Lives Therapy allows us to explore new areas of the unconscious mind in a new way. Its aim is the aim of all therapy: to help the patient define his view of the world, and to eliminate from it the extraneous fear, anxiety, and depression that come not from the outside, but from the deep reaches of the unconscious.

I do not expect people raised in the Western culture to accept reincarnation readily, as nearly a billion Eastern people do. We are too pragmatic, too practical, too skeptical to consider belief without hard evidence. Most of us insist that our beliefs deliver material assets to our lives. Sadly, we in this society have little use for the unmeasurable.

Because I believe that a therapist should use no techniques, no therapeutic approaches that cannot be incorporated into his own life, I must end by saying that I have come to live my life in a manner which reflects the basic precepts of this book. I am pleased to say to any and all who ask—it works.

BIBLIOGRAPHY

Cohen, Daniel. *The Mysteries of Reincarnation.* New York: Dodd, Mead & Co., 1975.

Moody, Raymond A., Jr., M.D. *Life After Life.* New York: Bantam Books, 1976.

Shiffrin, Nancy. "Past Lives, Present Problems." *Human Behavior Magazine.* Volume VI, No. 9. September 1977.

Stevenson, Ian, M.D. *Twenty Cases Suggestive of Reincarnation.* Charlottesville: University Press of Virginia, 1974.

Wambach, Helen. "Past Life Recall." *Psychic Magazine* (now *New Realities Magazine*). Volume VII, No. 5. November/December 1976.

Wambach, Helen. "Life Before Life." *Psychic Magazine* (now *New Realities Magazine*). Volume VII, No. 7. January/February 1977.